# THE
# SCEPTRED FLUTE
# SONGS OF INDIA

*The Golden Threshold,*
*The Bird of Time*
*& The Broken Wing*

*By*

## SAROJINI NAIDU

WITH A CHAPTER FROM
*Studies of Contemporary Poets*
BY MARY C. STURGEON

First published in 1943

# CONTENTS

# POEMS

# THE BIRD OF TIME

## SONGS OF LOVE AND DEATH

## SONGS OF THE SPRINGTIME

## INDIAN FOLK-SONGS
## TO INDIAN TUNES

## SONGS OF LIFE

## THE BROKEN WING

### SONGS OF LIFE AND DEATH

### MEMORIAL VERSES

# THE TEMPLE,
## A PILGRAMAGE OF LOVE

### I. THE GATE OF DELIGHT

### II. THE PATH OF TEARS

### III. THE SANCTUARY

# Sarojini Naidu

By Mary C. Sturgeon

Mrs Naidu is one of the two Indian poets who within the last few years have produced remarkable English poetry. The second of the two is, of course, Rabindranath Tagore, whose work has come to us a little later, who has published more, and whose recent visit to this country has brought him more closely under the public eye. Mrs Naidu is not so well known; but she deserves to be, for although the bulk of her work is not so large, its quality, so far as it can be compared with that of her compatriot, will easily bear the test. It is, however, so different in kind, and reveals a genius so contrasting, that one is piqued by an apparent problem. How is it that two children of what we are pleased to call the changeless East, under conditions nearly identical, should have produced results which are so different?

Both of these poets are lyrists born; both come of an old and distinguished Bengali ancestry; in both the culture of East and West are happily met; and both are working in the same artistic medium. Yet the poetry of Rabindranath Tagore is mystical, philosophic, and contemplative, remaining oriental therefore to that degree; and permitting a doubt of the *Quarterly* reviewer's dictum that "Gitanjali"is a synthesis of western and oriental elements. The complete synthesis would seem to rest with Mrs Naidu, whose poetry, though truly native to her motherland, is more sensuous than mystical, human and passionate rather than spiritual, and reveals a mentality more active than contemplative. Her affiliation with the Occident is so much the more complete; but her Eastern origin is never in doubt.

The themes of her verse and their setting are derived from

11

her own country. But her thought, with something of the energy of the strenuous West and something of its 'divine discontent,' plays upon the surface of an older and deeper calm which is her birthright. So, in her "Salutation to the Eternal Peace," she sings

> What care I for the world's loud weariness,
> Who dream in twilight granaries
> Thou dost bless
> With delicate sheaves of mellow silences?

Two distinguished poet-friends of Mrs Naidu—Mr Edmund Gosse and Mr Arthur Symons—have introduced her two principal volumes of verse with interesting biographical notes. The facts thus put in our possession convey a picture to the mind which is instantly recognizable in the poems.

A gracious and glowing personality appears, quick and warm with human feeling, exquisitely sensitive to beauty and receptive of ideas, wearing its culture, old and new, scientific and humane, with simplicity; but, as Mr Symons says, "a spirit of too much fire in too frail a body," and one moreover who has suffered and fought to the limit of human endurance.

We hear of birth and childhood in Hyderabad; of early scientific training by a father whose great learning was matched by his public spirit: of a first poem at the age of eleven, written in an impulse of reaction when a sum in algebra 'would not come right': of coming to England at the age of sixteen with a scholarship from the Nizam college; and of three years spent here, studying at King's College, London, and at Girton, with glorious intervals of holiday in Italy.

We hear, too, of a love-story that would make an idyll; of passion so strong and a will so resolute as almost to be incredible in such a delicate creature; of a marriage in defiance of caste, a few years of brilliant happiness and then a tragedy. And all through, as a dark background to the adventurous romance of her life, there is the shadow of weakness and ill-health. That shadow creeps into her poems, impressively, now and then. Indeed, if it were lacking, the bright oriental colouring would be almost too vivid. So, apart from its psychological and human interest, we may be thankful for such a poem as "To the God of Pain." It softens and deepens the final impression of the work.

> For thy dark altars, balm nor milk nor rice,
> But mine own soul thou'st ta'en for sacrifice.

The poem is purely subjective, of course, as is the still more moving piece, "The Poet to Death," in the same volume.

> Tarry a while, till I am satisfied
> Of love and grief, of earth and altering sky;
> Till all my human hungers are fulfilled,
> O Death, I cannot die!

We know that that is a cry out of actual and repeated experience; and from that point of view alone it has poignant interest. But what are we to say about the spirit of it—the philosophy which is implicit in it? Here is an added value of a higher kind, evidence of a mind which has taken its own stand upon reality, and which has no easy consolations when confronting the facts of existence. For this mind, neither the religions of East nor West are allowed to veil the truth; neither the hope of Nirvana nor the promise of Paradise may drug her sense of the value of life nor darken her perception of the beauty of phenomena. Resignation and renunciation are alike impossible to this ardent being who loves the earth so passionately; but the 'sternly scientific' nature of that early training—the description is her own—has made futile regret impossible, too. She has entered into full possession of the thought of our time; and strongly individual as she is, she has evolved for herself, to use her own words, a "subtle philosophy of living from moment to moment." That is no shallow epicureanism, however, for as she sings in a poem contrasting our changeful life with the immutable peace of the Buddha on his lotus-throne—

Nought shall conquer or control
The heavenward hunger of our soul.

It is as though, realizing that the present is the only moment of which we are certain, she had determined to crowd that moment to the utmost limit of living.

From such a philosophy, materialism of a nobler kind, one would expect a love of the concrete and tangible, a delight in sense impressions, and quick and strong emotion. Those are, in fact, the characteristics of much of the poetry in these two volumes, *The Golden Threshold* and *The Bird of Time*. The beauty of the material world, of line and especially of colour, is caught and recorded joyously. Life is regarded mainly from the outside, in action, or as a pageant; as an interesting event or a picturesque group. It is not often brooded over, and reflection is generally evident in but the lightest touches. The proportion of strictly subjective verse is small, and is not, on the whole, the finest work technically.

The introspective note seems unfavourable to Mrs Naidu's art: naturally so, one would conclude, from the buoyant temperament that is revealed. The love-songs are perhaps an exception, for one or two, which (as we know) treat fragments of the poet's own story, are fine in idea and in technique alike. There is, for example, "An Indian Love Song," in the first stanza of which the lover begs for his lady's love. But she reminds him of the barriers of caste between them; she is afraid to profane the laws of her father's creed; and her lover's kinsmen, in times past, have broken the altars of her people and slaughtered their sacred kine. The lover replies:

What are the sins of my race, Beloved, what are my
  people to thee?
And what are thy shrine, and kine and kindred, what are
  thy gods to me?
Love recks not of feuds and bitter follies, of stranger,
  comrade orkin,
Alike in his ear sound the temple bells and the cry of
  the muezzin.

There is also in the second volume the "Dirge," in which the
poet mourns the death of the husband whom she had dared to
marry against the laws of caste; and which almost unconsciously
reveals the influence of centuries of Suttee upon the mind of
Indian womanhood.

Shatter her shining bracelets, break the string
Threading the mystic marriage-beads that cling
Loth to desert a sobbing throat so sweet,
Unbind the golden anklets on her feet,
Divest her of her azure veils and cloud
Her living beauty in a living shroud.

Even here, however, the effect is gained by colour and
movement; by the grouping of images rather than by the
development of an idea; and that will be found to be Mrs Naidu's
method in the many delightful lyrics of these volumes where
she is most successful. The "Folk Songs" of her first book are an
example. One assumes that they are early work, partly because
they are the first group in the earlier of the two volumes; but
more particularly because they adopt so literally the advice
which Mr Edmund Gosse gave her at the beginning of her career.
When she came as a girl to England and was a student of London
University at King's College, she submitted to Mr Gosse a bundle
of manuscript poems. He describes them as accurate and careful

work, but too derivative; modelled too palpably on the great poets of the previous generation. His advice, therefore, was that they should be destroyed, and that the author should start afresh upon native themes and in her own manner. The counsel was exactly followed: the manuscript went into the wastepaper basket, and the poet set to work on what we cannot doubt is this first group of songs made out of the lives of her own people.

There is all the hemisphere between these lyrics and those of late-Victorian England. Here we find a "Village Song" of a mother to the little bride who is still all but a baby; and to whom the fairies call so insistently that she will not stay "for bridal songs and bridal cakes and sandal-scented leisure." In the song of the "Palanquin Bearers" we positively see the lithe and rhythmic movements which bear some Indian beauty along, lightly "as a pearl on a string." And there is a song written to one of the tunes of those native minstrels who wander, free and wild as the wind, singing of

> The sword of old battles, the crown of old kings,
> And happy and simple and sorrowful things.

The "Harvest Hymn" raises thanksgiving for strange bounties to gods of unfamiliar names; and the "Cradle Song" evokes a tropical night, heavy with scent and drenched with dew—

> Sweet, shut your eyes,
> The wild fire-flies
> Dance through the fairy *neem*;
> From the poppy-bole,For you I stole
> A little, lovely dream.

In its lightness and grace, this poem is one of the exquisite things in our language: one of the little lyric flights, like William Watson's "April," which in their clear sweetness and apparent spontaneity are like some small bird's song. Mrs Naidu has said of herself—"I sing just as the birds do"; and as regards her loveliest lyrics (there are a fair proportion of them) she speaks a larger truth than she meant. Their simplicity and abandonment to the sheer joy of singing are infinitely refreshing; and fragile though they seem, one suspects them of great vitality. In the later volume there is another called "Golden Cassia"—the bright blooms that her people call mere 'woodland flowers.' The poet has other fancies about them; sometimes they seem to her like fragments of a fallen star—

> Or golden lamps for a fairy shrine,
> Or golden pitchers for fairy wine.
>
> Perchance you are, O frail and sweet!
> Bright anklet-bells from the wild spring's feet,
>
> Or the gleaming tears that some fair bride shed
> Remembering her lost maidenhead.

The tenderness and delicacy of verse like that might mislead us. We might suppose that the qualities of Mrs Naidu's work were only those which are arbitrarily known as feminine. But this poet, like Mrs Browning, is faithful to her own sensuous and passionate temperament. She has not timidly sheltered behind a convention which, because some women-poets have been austere, prescribes austerity, neutral tones, and a pale light for the woman-artist in this sphere. And, as a result, we have all the evidence of a richly-dowered sensibility responding frankly to the vivid light and colour, the liberal contours and rich scents and great spaces of the world she loves; and responding no less warmly and freely to human instincts. Occasionally her verse achieves the expression of sheer sensuous ecstasy. It does that, perhaps, in the two Dance poems—from the very reason that her art is so true and free. The theme requires exactly that treatment; and in "Indian Dancers" there is besides a curiously successful union between the measure that is employed and the subject of the poem—

> Their glittering garments of purple are burning like
>    tremulous dawns inthe quivering air,
> And exquisite, subtle and slow are the tinkle and tread
>    of their rhythmical, slumber-soft feet.

The love-songs, though in many moods, are always the frank expression of emotion that is deep and strong. One that is especially beautiful is the utterance of a young girl who, while her sisters prepare the rites for a religious festival, stands aside with folded hands dreaming of her lover. She is secretly asking herself what need has she to supplicate the gods, being blessed by love; and again, in the couple of stanzas called "Ecstasy," the rapture has passed, by its very intensity, into pain.

> Shelter my soul, O my love!
>    My soul is bent low with the pain
> And the burden of love, like the grace
>    Of a flower that is smitten with rain:
> O shelter my soul from thy face!

But, when all is said, it is the life of her people which inspires this poet most perfectly. In the lighter lyrics one sees the fineness of her touch; and in the love-poems the depth of her passion. But, in the folk-songs, all the qualities of her genius have contributed. Grace and tenderness have been reinforced by an observant eye, broad sympathy and a capacity for thought which reveals itself not so much as a systematic process as an atmosphere, suffusing the poems with gentle pensiveness. And always the artistic method is that of picking out the theme in bright sharp lines, and presenting the idea concretely, through the grouping of picturesque facts. There is a poem called "Street Cries" which is a vivid bit of the life of an Eastern city. First we have early morning, when the workers hurry out, fasting, to their toil; and the cry 'Buy bread, Buy bread' rings down the eager street; then midday, hot and thirsty, when the cry is 'Buy fruit, Buy fruit'; and finally, evening.

> When twinkling twilight o'er the gay bazaars,
> Unfurls a sudden canopy of stars,
> When lutes are strung and fragrant torches lit
> On white roof-terraces where lovers sit
> Drinking together of life's poignant sweet,
> *Buy flowers, buy flowers*, floats down the singing street.

Another of these shining pictures will be found in "Nightfall in the City of Hyderabad," Mrs Naidu's own city; and again in the song called "In a Latticed Balcony." But there are several others in which, added to the suggestion of an old civilization and strange customs, there is a haunting sense of things older and stranger still. Of such is this one, called "Indian Weavers."

> Weavers, weaving at break of day,
> Why do you weave a garment so gay? . . .
> Blue as the wing of a halcyon wild,
> We weave the robes of a new-born child.

> Weavers, weaving solemn and still,
> Why do you weave in the moonlight chill? . . .
> White as a feather and white as a cloud,
> We weave a dead man's funeral shroud.

A Chapter from
*Studies of Contemporary Poets*, 1916

# THE
# GOLDEN THRESHOLD

# FOLK SONGS

## PALANQUIN BEARERS

―――――――――――――

LIGHTLY, O lightly we bear her along,
She sways like a flower in the wind of our song;
She skims like a bird on the foam of a stream,
She floats like a laugh from the lips of a dream.
Gaily, O gaily we glide and we sing,
We bear her along like a pearl on a string.

Softly, O softly we bear her along,
She hangs like a star in the dew of our song;
She springs like a beam on the brow of the tide,
She falls like a tear from the eyes of a bride.
Lightly, O lightly we glide and we sing,
We bear her along like a pearl on a string.

# WANDERING SINGERS

---

(Written to one of their Tunes)

WHERE the voice of the wind calls our wandering feet,
Through echoing forest and echoing street,
With lutes in our hands ever-singing we roam,
All men are our kindred, the world is our home.

Our lays are of cities whose lustre is shed,
The laughter and beauty of women long dead;
The sword of old battles, the crown of old kings,
And happy and simple and sorrowful things.

What hope shall we gather, what dreams shall we sow?
Where the wind calls our wandering footsteps we go.
No love bids us tarry, no joy bids us wait:
The voice of the wind is the voice of our fate.

# INDIAN WEAVERS

WEAVERS, weaving at break of day,
Why do you weave a garment so gay? . . .
Blue as the wing of a halcyon wild,
We weave the robes of a new-born child.

Weavers, weaving at fall of night,
Why do you weave a garment so bright? . . .
Like the plumes of a peacock, purple and green,
We weave the marriage-veils of a queen.

Weavers, weaving solemn and still,
What do you weave in the moonlight chill? . . .
White as a feather and white as a cloud,
We weave a dead man's funeral shroud.

# COROMANDEL FISHERS

RISE, brothers, rise, the wakening skies pray
    to the morning light,
The wind lies asleep in the arms of the dawn
    like a child that has cried all night.
Come, let us gather our nets from the shore,
    and set our catamarans free,
To capture the leaping wealth of the tide, for
    we are the sons of the sea.

No longer delay, let us hasten away in the
    track of the sea-gull's call,
The sea is our mother, the cloud is our brother,
    the waves are our comrades all.
What though we toss at the fall of the sun
    where the hand of the sea-god drives?
He who holds the storm by the hair, will hide
    in his breast our lives.

Sweet is the shade of the cocoanut glade, and
    the scent of the mango grove,
And sweet are the sands at the full o' the moon with the
    sound of the voices we love.
But sweeter, O brothers, the kiss of the spray
    and the dance of the wild foam's glee:
Row, brothers, row to the blue of the verge,
    where the low sky mates with the sea.

# THE SNAKE-CHARMER

WHITHER dost thou hide from the magic of my flute-call?
In what moonlight-tangled meshes of perfume,
Where the clustering keovas guard the squirrel's slumber,
Where the deep woods glimmer with the jasmine's bloom?

I'll feed thee, O beloved, on milk and wild red honey,
I'll bear thee in a basket of rushes, green and white,
To a palace-bower where golden-vested maidens
Thread with mellow laughter the petals of delight.

Whither dost thou loiter, by what murmuring hollows,
Where oleanders scatter their ambrosial fire?
Come, thou subtle bride of my mellifluous wooing,
Come, thou silver-breasted moonbeam of desire!

# CORN-GRINDERS

*O little mouse, why dost thou cry*
*While merry stars laugh in the sky?*

Alas! alas! my lord is dead!
Ah, who will ease my bitter pain?
He went to seek a millet-grain
In the rich farmer's granary shed;
They caught him in a baited snare,
And slew my lover unaware:
Alas! alas! my lord is dead.

*O little deer, why dost thou moan,*
*Hid in thy forest-bower alone?*

Alas! alas! my lord is dead!
Ah! who will quiet my lament?
At fall of eventide he went
To drink beside the river-head;
A waiting hunter threw his dart,
And struck my lover through the heart.
Alas! alas! my lord is dead.

*O little bride, why dost thou weep*
*With all the happy world asleep?*

Alas! alas! my lord is dead!
Ah, who will stay these hungry tears,
Or still the want of famished years,
And crown with love my marriage-bed?
My soul burns with the quenchless fire
That lit my lover's funeral pyre:
Alas! alas! my lord is dead.

# VILLAGE-SONG

HONEY, child, honey, child, whither are you going?
Would you cast your jewels all to the breezes blowing?
Would you leave the mother who on golden grain has fed you?
Would you grieve the lover who is riding forth to wed you?

Mother mine, to the wild forest I am going,
Where upon the champa boughs the champa buds are blowing;
To the koil-haunted river-isles where lotus lilies glisten,
The voices of the fairy folk are calling me: O listen!

Honey, child, honey, child, the world is full of pleasure,
Of bridal-songs and cradle-songs and sandal-scented leisure.
Your bridal robes are in the loom, silver and saffron glowing,
Your bridal cakes are on the hearth: O whither are you going?

The bridal-songs and cradle-songs have cadences of sorrow,
The laughter of the sun to-day, the wind of death to-morrow.
Far sweeter sound the forest-notes where forest-streams are
    falling;
O mother mine, I cannot stay, the fairy-folk are calling.

# IN PRAISE OF HENNA

---

A KOKILA called from a henna-spray:
*Lira! Liree! Lira! Liree!*
Hasten, maidens, hasten away
To gather the leaves of the henna-tree.
Send your pitchers afloat on the tide,
Gather the leaves ere the dawn be old,
Grind them in mortars of amber and gold,
The fresh green leaves of the henna-tree.

A kokila called from a henna-spray:
*Lira! Liree! Lira! Liree!*
Hasten maidens, hasten away
To gather the leaves of the henna-tree.
The tilka's red for the brow of a bride,
And betel-nut's red for lips that are sweet;
But, for lily-like fingers and feet,
The red, the red of the henna-tree.

# HARVEST HYMN

---

*Men's Voices*

LORD of the lotus, lord of the harvest,
Bright and munificent lord of the morn!
Thine is the bounty that prospered our sowing,
Thine is the bounty that nurtured our corn.
We bring thee our songs and our garlands for tribute,
The gold of our fields and the gold of our fruit;
O giver of mellowing radiance, we hail thee,
We praise thee, O Surya, with cymbal and flute.

Lord of the rainbow, lord of the harvest,
Great and beneficent lord of the main!
Thine is the mercy that cherished our furrows,
Thine is the mercy that fostered our grain.
We bring thee our thanks and our garlands for tribute,
The wealth of our valleys, new-garnered and ripe;
O sender of rain and the dewfall, we hail thee,
We praise thee, Varuna, with cymbal and pipe.

*Women's Voices*

Queen of the gourd-flower, queen of the harvest,
Sweet and omnipotent mother, O Earth!
Thine is the plentiful bosom that feeds us,
Thine is the womb where our riches have birth.
We bring thee our love and our garlands for tribute,
With gifts of thy opulent giving we come;
O source of our manifold gladness, we hail thee,
We praise thee, O Prithvi, with cymbal and drum.


*All Voices*

Lord of the Universe, Lord of our being,
Father eternal, ineffable Om!
Thou art the Seed and the Scythe of our harvests,
Thou art our Hands and our Heart and our Home.
We bring thee our lives and our labours for tribute,
Grant us thy succour, thy counsel, thy care.
O Life of all life and all blessing, we hail thee,
We praise thee, O Bramha, with cymbal and prayer.

# INDIAN LOVE-SONG

───────────────

*She*

LIKE a serpent to the calling voice of flutes,
Glides my heart into thy fingers, O my Love!
Where the night-wind, like a lover, leans above
His jasmine-gardens and sirisha-bowers;
And on ripe boughs of many-coloured fruits
Bright parrots cluster like vermilion flowers.

*He*

Like the perfume in the petals of a rose,
Hides thy heart within my bosom, O my love!
Like a garland, like a jewel, like a dove
That hangs its nest in the asoka-tree.
Lie still, O love, until the morning sows
Her tents of gold on fields of ivory.

# CRADLE-SONG

FROM groves of spice,
　O'er fields of rice,
Athwart the lotus-stream,
　　I bring for you,
　　Aglint with dew
A little lovely dream.

　Sweet, shut your eyes,
　The wild fire-flies
Dance through the fairy neem;
　　From the poppy-bole
　　For you I stole
A little lovely dream.

　Dear eyes, good-night,
　In golden light
The stars around you gleam;
　　On you I press
　　With soft caress
A little lovely dream.

# SUTTEE

LAMP of my life, the lips of Death
Hath blown thee out with their sudden breath;
Naught shall revive thy vanished spark . . .
Love, must I dwell in the living dark?

Tree of my life, Death's cruel foot
Hath crushed thee down to thy hidden root;
Nought shall restore thy glory fled . . .
Shall the blossom live when the tree is dead?

Life of my life, Death's bitter sword
Hath severed us like a broken word,
Rent us in twain who are but one . .
Shall the flesh survive when the soul is gone?

# SONGS FOR MUSIC

## SONG OF A DREAM

---

ONCE in the dream of a night I stood
Lone in the light of a magical wood,
Soul-deep in visions that poppy-like sprang;
And spirits of Truth were the birds that sang,
And spirits of Love were the stars that glowed,
And spirits of Peace were the streams that flowed
In that magical wood in the land of sleep.

Lone in the light of that magical grove,
I felt the stars of the spirits of Love
Gather and gleam round my delicate youth,
And I heard the song of the spirits of Truth;
To quench my longing I bent me low
By the streams of the spirits of Peace that flow
In that magical wood in the land of sleep.

# HUMAYUN TO ZOBEIDA

(From the Urdu)

You flaunt your beauty in the rose, your glory in the dawn,
Your sweetness in the nightingale, your whiteness in the swan.

You haunt my waking like a dream, my slumber like a moon,
Pervade me like a musky scent, possess me like a tune.

Yet, when I crave of you, my sweet, one tender moment's grace,
You cry, "*I sit behind the veil, I cannot show my face.*"

Shall any foolish veil divide my longing from my bliss?
Shall any fragile curtain hide your beauty from my kiss?

What war is this of *Thee* and *Me*? Give o'er the wanton strife,
You are the heart within my heart, the life within my life.

# AUTUMN SONG

LIKE a joy on the heart of a sorrow,
    The sunset hangs on a cloud;
A golden storm of glittering sheaves,
Of fair and frail and fluttering leaves,
    The wild wind blows in a cloud.

Hark to a voice that is calling
    To my heart in the voice of the wind:
My heart is weary and sad and alone,
For its dreams like the fluttering leaves have gone,
    And why should I stay behind?

# ALABASTER

LIKE this alabaster box whose art
Is frail as a cassia-flower, is my heart,
Carven with delicate dreams and wrought
With many a subtle and exquisite thought.

Therein I treasure the spice and scent
Of rich and passionate memories blent
Like odours of cinnamon, sandal and clove,
Of song and sorrow and life and love.

# ECSTASY

COVER mine eyes, O my Love!
Mine eyes that are weary of bliss
As of light that is poignant and strong
O silence my lips with a kiss,
My lips that are weary of song!

Shelter my soul, O my love!
My soul is bent low with the pain
And the burden of love, like the grace
Of a flower that is smitten with rain:
O shelter my soul from thy face!

# TO MY FAIRY FANCIES

NAY, no longer I may hold you,
   In my spirit's soft caresses,
Nor like lotus-leaves enfold you
   In the tangles of my tresses.
Fairy fancies, fly away
    To the white cloud-wildernesses,
      Fly away!

Nay, no longer ye may linger
   With your laughter-lighted faces,
Now I am a thought-worn singer
   In life's high and lonely places.
Fairy fancies, fly away,
    To bright wind-inwoven spaces,
      Fly away!

# POEMS

## ODE TO H.H.
## THE NIZAM OF HYDERABAD

———————

(Presented at the Ramzan Durbar)

DEIGN, Prince, my tribute to receive,
This lyric offering to your name,
Who round your jewelled scepter bind
The lilies of a poet's fame;
Beneath whose sway concordant dwell
The peoples whom your laws embrace,
In brotherhood of diverse creeds,
And harmony of diverse race:

The votaries of the Prophet's faith,
Of whom you are the crown and chief
And they, who bear on Vedic brows
Their mystic symbols of belief;

And they, who worshipping the sun,
Fled o'er the old Iranian sea;
And they, who bow to Him who trod
The midnight waves of Galilee.

Sweet, sumptuous fables of Baghdad
The splendours of your court recall,
The torches of a Thousand Nights
Blaze through a single festival;
And Saki-singers down the streets,
Pour for us, in a stream divine,
From goblets of your love-ghazals
The rapture of your Sufi wine.

Prince, where your radiant cities smile,
Grim hills their sombre vigils keep,
Your ancient forests hoard and hold
The legends of their centuried sleep;
Your birds of peace white-pinioned float
O'er ruined fort and storied plain,
Your faithful stewards sleepless guard
The harvests of your gold and grain.

God give you joy, God give you grace
To shield the truth and smite the wrong,
To honour Virtue, Valour, Worth.
To cherish faith and foster song.
So may the lustre of your days
Outshine the deeds Firdusi sung,
Your name within a nation's prayer,
Your music on a nation's tongue.

# LEILI

---

THE serpents are asleep among the poppies,
The fireflies light the soundless panther's way
To tangled paths where shy gazelles are straying,
And parrot-plumes outshine the dying day.
O soft! the lotus-buds upon the stream
Are stirring like sweet maidens when they dream.

A caste-mark on the azure brows of Heaven,
The golden moon burns sacred, solemn, bright
The winds are dancing in the forest-temple,
And swooning at the holy feet of Night.
Hush! in the silence mystic voices sing
And make the gods their incense-offering.

# IN THE FOREST

HERE, O my heart, let us burn the dear dreams that are dead,
Here in this wood let us fashion a funeral pyre
Of fallen white petals and leaves that are mellow and red,
Here let us burn them in noon's flaming torches of fire.

We are weary, my heart, we are weary, so long we have borne
The heavy loved burden of dreams that are dead, let us rest,
Let us scatter their ashes away, for a while let us mourn;
We will rest, O my heart, till the shadows are gray in the west.

But soon we must rise, O my heart, we must wander again
Into the war of the world and the strife of the throng;
Let us rise, O my heart, let us gather the dreams that remain,
We will conquer the sorrow of life with the sorrow of song.

# PAST AND FUTURE

*The new hath come and now the old retires:*
And so the past becomes a mountain-cell,
Where lone, apart, old hermit-memories dwell
In consecrated calm, forgotten yet
Of the keen heart that hastens to forget
Old longings in fulfilling new desires.

And now the Soul stands in a vague, intense
Expectancy and anguish of suspense,
On the dim chamber-threshold . . . lo! he sees
Like a strange, fated bride as yet unknown,
His timid future shrinking there alone,
Beneath her marriage-veil of mysteries.

# LIFE

———————————

CHILDREN, ye have not lived, to you it seems
Life is a lovely stalactite of dreams,
Or carnival of careless joys that leap
About your hearts like billows on the deep
In flames of amber and of amethyst.

Children, ye have not lived, ye but exist
Till some resistless hour shall rise and move
Your hearts to wake and hunger after love,
And thirst with passionate longing for the things
That burn your brows with blood-red sufferings.

Till ye have battled with great grief and fears,
And borne the conflict of dream-shattering years,
Wounded with fierce desire and worn with strife,
Children, ye have not lived: for this is life.

# THE POET'S LOVE-SONG

In noon-tide hours, O Love, secure and strong,
   I need thee not; mad dreams are mine to bind
   The world to my desire, and hold the wind
A voiceless captive to my conquering song.
   I need thee not, I am content with these:
   Keep silence in thy soul, beyond the seas!

But in the desolate hour of midnight, when
   An ecstasy of starry silence sleeps
   On the still mountains and the soundless deeps,
And my soul hungers for thy voice, O then,
   Love, like the magic of wild melodies,
   Let thy soul answer mine across the seas.

# TO THE GOD OF PAIN

UNWILLING priestess in thy cruel fane,
Long hast thou held me, pitiless god of Pain,
Bound to thy worship by reluctant vows,
My tired breast girt with suffering, and my brows
Anointed with perpetual weariness.
Long have I borne thy service, through the stress
Of rigorous years, sad days and slumberless nights,
Performing thine inexorable rites.

For thy dark altars, balm nor milk nor rice,
But mine own soul thou'st ta'en for sacrifice:
All the rich honey of my youth's desire,
And all the sweet oils from my crushed life drawn,
And all my flower-like dreams and gem-like fire
Of hopes up-leaping like the light of dawn.

I have no more to give, all that was mine
Is laid, a wrested tribute, at thy shrine;
Let me depart, for my whole soul is wrung,
And all my cheerless orisons are sung;
Let me depart, with faint limbs let me creep
To some dim shade and sink me down to sleep.

# THE SONG OF PRINCESS ZEB-UN-NISSA IN PRAISE OF HER OWN BEAUTY

───────────

(From the Persian)

WHEN from my cheek I lift my veil,
The roses turn with envy pale,
　　And from their pierced hearts, rich with pain,
Send forth their fragrance like a wail.

Or if perchance one perfumed tress
Be lowered to the wind's caress,
　　The honeyed hyacinths complain,
And languish in a sweet distress.

And, when I pause, still groves among,
(Such loveliness is mine) a throng
　　Of nightingales awake and strain
Their souls into a quivering song.

# INDIAN DANCERS

EYES ravished with rapture, celestially panting, what
    passionate bosoms aflaming with fire
Drink deep of the hush of the hyacinth heavens that
    glimmer around them in fountains of light;
O wild and entrancing the strain of keen music that
    cleaveth the stars like a wail of desire,
And beautiful dancers with houri-like faces bewitch the
    voluptuous watches of night.

The scents of red roses and sandalwood flutter and die
    in the maze of their gem-tangled hair,
And smiles are entwining like magical serpents the
    poppies of lips that are opiate-sweet;
Their glittering garments of purple are burning like
    tremulous dawns in the quivering air,
And exquisite, subtle and slow are the tinkle and tread
    of their rhythmical, slumber-soft feet.

Now silent, now singing and swaying and swinging,
    like blossoms that bend to the breezes or showers,
Now wantonly winding, they flash, now they falter,
    and, lingering, languish in radiant choir;
Their jewel-girt arms and warm, wavering, lily-long
    fingers enchant through melodious hours,
Eyes ravished with rapture, celestially panting, what
    passionate bosoms aflaming with fire!

# MY DEAD DREAM

HAVE you found me, at last, O my Dream?
   Seven aeons ago
You died and I buried you deep under forests of snow.
Why have you come hither? Who bade you
   awake from your sleep
And track me beyond the cerulean foam of the deep?

Would you tear from my lintels these sacred green
   garlands of leaves?
Would you scare the white, nested, wild pigeons
   of joy from my eaves?
Would you touch and defile with dead fingers the
   robes of my priest?
Would you weave your dim moan with the chantings
   of love at my feast?

Go back to your grave, O my Dream, under forests
   of snow,
Where a heart-riven child hid you once, seven
   aeons ago.
Who bade you arise from your darkness? I bid
   you depart!
Profane not the shrines I have raised in the
   clefts of my heart.

# DAMAYANTE TO NALA
# IN THE HOUR OF EXILE

---

(A fragment)

SHALT thou be conquered of a human fate
My liege, my lover, whose imperial head
Hath never bent in sorrow of defeat?
Shalt thou be vanquished, whose imperial feet
Have shattered armies and stamped empires dead?
Who shall unking thee, husband of a queen?
Wear thou thy majesty inviolate.
Earth's glories flee of human eyes unseen,
Earth's kingdoms fade to a remembered dream,
But thine henceforth shall be a power supreme,
Dazzling command and rich dominion,
The winds thy heralds and thy vassals all
The silver-belted planets and the sun.
Where'er the radiance of thy coming fall,
Shall dawn for thee her saffron footcloths spread,
Sunset her purple canopies and red,
In serried splendour, and the night unfold
Her velvet darkness wrought with starry gold
For kingly raiment, soft as cygnet-down.
My hair shall braid thy temples like a crown
Of sapphires, and my kiss upon thy brows
Like cithar-music lull thee to repose,
Till the sun yield thee homage of his light.

O king, thy kingdom who from thee can wrest?
What fate shall dare uncrown thee from this breast,
O god-born lover, whom my love doth gird
And armour with impregnable delight
Of Hope's triumphant keen flame-carven sword?

# THE QUEEN'S RIVAL

---

## I

QUEEN GULNAAR sat on her ivory bed,
Around her countless treasures were spread;

Her chamber walls were richly inlaid
With agate, porphory, onyx and jade;

The tissues that veiled her delicate breast,
Glowed with the hues of a lapwing's crest;

But still she gazed in her mirror and sighed
"O King, my heart is unsatisfied."

King Feroz bent from his ebony seat:
"Is thy least desire unfulfilled, O Sweet?

"Let thy mouth speak and my life be spent
To clear the sky of thy discontent."

"I tire of my beauty, I tire of this
Empty splendour and shadowless bliss;

"With none to envy and none gainsay,
No savour or salt hath my dream or day."

Queen Gulnaar sighed like a murmuring rose:
"Give me a rival, O King Feroz."

## II

King Feroz spoke to his Chief Vizier:
"Lo! ere to-morrow's dawn be here,

"Send forth my messengers over the sea,
To seek seven beautiful brides for me;

"Radiant of feature and regal of mien,
Seven handmaids meet for the Persian Queen."

\* \* \* \* \*

Seven new moon tides at the Vesper call,
King Feroz led to Queen Gulnaar's hall

A young queen eyed like the morning star:
"I bring thee a rival, O Queen Gulnaar."

But still she gazed in her mirror and sighed:
"O King, my heart is unsatisfied."

Seven queens shone round her ivory bed,
Like seven soft gems on a silken thread,

Like seven fair lamps in a royal tower,
Like seven bright petals of Beauty's flower

Queen Gulnaar sighed like a murmuring rose
"Where is my rival, O King Feroz?"

## III

When spring winds wakened the mountain floods,
And kindled the flame of the tulip buds,

When bees grew loud and the days grew long,
And the peach groves thrilled to the oriole's song,

Queen Gulnaar sat on her ivory bed,
Decking with jewels her exquisite head;

And still she gazed in her mirror and sighed:
"O King, my heart is unsatisfied."

Queen Gulnaar's daughter two spring times old,
In blue robes bordered with tassels of gold,

Ran to her knee like a wildwood fay,
And plucked from her hand the mirror away.

Quickly she set on her own light curls
Her mother's fillet with fringes of pearls;

Quickly she turned with a child's caprice
And pressed on the mirror a swift, glad kiss.

Queen Gulnaar laughed like a tremulous rose:
"Here is my rival, O King Feroz."

# THE POET TO DEATH

TARRY a while, O Death, I cannot die
While yet my sweet life burgeons with its spring;
Fair is my youth, and rich the echoing boughs
Where *dhadikulas* sing.

Tarry a while, O Death, I cannot die
With all my blossoming hopes unharvested,
My joys ungarnered, all my songs unsung,
And all my tears unshed.

Tarry a while, till I am satisfied
Of love and grief, of earth and altering sky;
Till all my human hungers are fulfilled,
O Death, I cannot die!

# THE INDIAN GIPSY

In tattered robes that hoard a glittering trace
Of bygone colours, broidered to the knee,
Behold her, daughter of a wandering race,
Tameless, with the bold falcon's agile grace,
And the lithe tiger's sinuous majesty.

With frugal skill her simple wants she tends,
She folds her tawny heifers and her sheep
On lonely meadows when the daylight ends,
Ere the quick night upon her flock descends
Like a black panther from the caves of sleep.

Time's river winds in foaming centuries
Its changing, swift, irrevocable course
To far off and incalculable seas;
She is twin-born with primal mysteries,
And drinks of life at Time's forgotten source.

# TO MY CHILDREN

---

### *Jaya Surya, aetat 4*

GOLDEN sun of victory, born
In my life's unclouded morn,
In my lambent sky of love,
May your growing glory prove
Sacred to your consecration,
To my heart and to my nation.
Sun of victory, may you be
Sun of song and liberty.

### *Padmaja, aetat 3*

Lotus-maiden, you who claim
All the sweetness of your name,
Lakshmi, fortune's queen, defend you,
Lotus-born like you, and send you
Balmy moons of love to bless you,
Gentle joy-winds to caress you.
Lotus-maiden, may you be
Fragrant of all ecstasy.

*Ranadheera, aetat 2*

Little lord of battle, hail
In your newly-tempered mail!
Learn to conquer, learn to fight
In the foremost flanks of right,
Like Valmiki's heroes bold,
Rubies girt in epic gold.
Lord of battle, may you be,
Lord of love and chivalry.

*Lilamani, aetat 1*

Limpid jewel of delight
Severed from the tender night
Of your sheltering mother-mine,
Leap and sparkle, dance and shine,
Blithely and securely set
In love's magic coronet.
Living jewel, may you be
Laughter-bound and sorrow-free.

# THE PARDAH NASHIN

HER life is a revolving dream
Of languid and sequestered ease;
Her girdles and her fillets gleam
Like changing fires on sunset seas;
Her raiment is like morning mist,
Shot opal, gold and amethyst.

From thieving light of eyes impure,
From coveting sun or wind's caress,
Her days are guarded and secure
Behind her carven lattices,
Like jewels in a turbaned crest,
Like secrets in a lover's breast.

But though no hand unsanctioned dares
Unveil the mysteries of her grace,
Time lifts the curtain unawares,
And Sorrow looks into her face . . .
Who shall prevent the subtle years,
Or shield a woman's eyes from tears?

# TO YOUTH

O YOUTH, sweet comrade Youth, wouldst thou be gone?
Long have we dwelt together, thou and I;
Together drunk of many an alien dawn,
And plucked the fruit of many an alien sky.

Ah, fickle friend, must I, who yesterday
Dreamed forwards to long, undimmed ecstasy,
Henceforward dream, because thou wilt not stay,
Backward to transient pleasure and to thee?

I give thee back thy false, ephemeral vow;
But, O beloved comrade, ere we part,
Upon my mournful eyelids and my brow
Kiss me who hold thine image in my heart.

## NIGHTFALL IN THE
## CITY OF HYDERABAD

---

SEE how the speckled sky burns like a pigeon's throat,
Jewelled with embers of opal and peridote.

See the white river that flashes and scintillates,
Curved like a tusk from the mouth of the city-gates.

Hark, from the minaret, how the muezzin's call
Floats like a battle-flag over the city wall.

From trellised balconies, languid and luminous
Faces gleam, veiled in a splendour voluminous.

Leisurely elephants wind through the winding lanes,
Swinging their silver bells hung from their silver chains.

Round the high Char Minar sounds of gay cavalcades
Blend with the music of cymbals and serenades.

Over the city bridge Night comes majestical,
Borne like a queen to a sumptuous festival.

# STREET CRIES

WHEN dawn's first cymbals beat upon the sky,
Rousing the world to labour's various cry,
To tend the flock, to bind the mellowing grain,
From ardent toil to forge a little gain,
And fasting men go forth on hurrying feet,
*buy bread, buy bread*, rings down the eager street.

When the earth falters and the waters swoon
With the implacable radiance of noon,
And in dim shelters koils hush their notes,
And the faint, thirsting blood in languid throats
Craves liquid succour from the cruel heat,
*buy fruit, buy fruit,* steals down the panting street.

When twilight twinkling o'er the gay bazaars,
Unfurls a sudden canopy of stars,
When lutes are strung and fragrant torches lit
On white roof-terraces where lovers sit
Drinking together of life's poignant sweet,
*Buy Flowers, Buy Flowers,* floats down the singing street.

# TO INDIA

O YOUNG through all thy immemorial years!
Rise, Mother, rise, regenerate from thy gloom,
And, like a bride high-mated with the spheres,
Beget new glories from thine ageless womb!

The nations that in fettered darkness weep
Crave thee to lead them where great mornings break . . .
Mother, O Mother, wherefore dost thou sleep?
Arise and answer for thy children's sake!

Thy Future calls thee with a manifold sound
To crescent honours, splendours, victories vast;
Waken, O slumbering Mother and be crowned,
Who once wert empress of the sovereign Past.

# THE ROYAL
# TOMBS OF GOLCONDA

---

I MUSE among these silent fanes
Whose spacious darkness guards your dust;
Around me sleep the hoary plains
That hold your ancient wars in trust.
I pause, my dreaming spirit hears,
Across the wind's unquiet tides,
The glimmering music of your spears,
The laughter of your royal brides.

In vain, O Kings, doth time aspire
To make your names oblivion's sport,
While yonder hill wears like a tier
The ruined grandeur of your fort.
Though centuries falter and decline,
Your proven strongholds shall remain
Embodied memories of your line,
Incarnate legends of your reign.

O Queens, in vain old Fate decreed
Your flower-like bodies to the tomb;
Death is in truth the vital seed
Of your imperishable bloom
Each new-born year the bulbuls sing
Their songs of your renascent loves;
Your beauty wakens with the spring
To kindle these pomegranate groves.

# TO A BUDDHA
# SEATED ON A LOTUS

---

LORD BUDDHA, on thy Lotus-throne,
With praying eyes and hands elate,
What mystic rapture dost thou own,
Immutable and ultimate?
What peace, unravished of our ken,
Annihilate from the world of men?

The wind of change for ever blows
Across the tumult of our way,
To-morrow's unborn griefs depose
The sorrows of our yesterday.
Dream yields to dream, strife follows strife,
And Death unweaves the webs of Life.

For us the travail and the heat,
The broken secrets of our pride,
The strenuous lessons of defeat,
The flower deferred, the fruit denied;
But not the peace, supremely won,
Lord Buddha, of thy Lotus-throne.

With futile hands we seek to gain
Our inaccessible desire,
Diviner summits to attain,
With faith that sinks and feet that tire;
But nought shall conquer or control
The heavenward hunger of our soul.

The end, elusive and afar,
Still lures us with its beckoning flight,
And all our mortal moments are
A session of the Infinite.
How shall we reach the great, unknown
Nirvana of thy Lotus-throne?

# THE BIRD OF TIME

# SONGS OF
# LOVE AND DEATH

## THE BIRD OF TIME

---

O Bird of Time on your fruitful bough
What are the songs you sing? . . .
Songs of the glory and gladness of life,
Of poignant sorrow and passionate strife,
And the lilting joy of the spring;
Of hope that sows for the years unborn,
And faith that dreams of a tarrying morn,
The fragrant peace of the twilight's breath,
And the mystic silence that men call death.

O Bird of Time, say where did you learn
The changing measures you sing? . . .
In blowing forests and breaking tides,
In the happy laughter of new-made brides,

And the nests of the new-born spring;
In the dawn that thrills to a mother's prayer,
And the night that shelters a heart's despair,
In the sigh of pity, the sob of hate,
And the pride of a soul that has conquered fate.

# DIRGE:

---

## IN SORROW OF HER BEREAVEMENT

WHAT longer need hath she of loveliness
Whom Death has parted from her lord's caress?
Of glimmering robes like rainbow-tangled mist,
Of gleaming glass or jewels on her wrist,
Blossoms or fillet-pearls to deck her head,
Or jasmine garlands to adorn her bed?

Put by the mirror of her bridal days. . .
Why needs she now its counsel or its praise,
Or happy symbol of the henna leaf
For hands that know the comradeship of grief,
Red spices for her lips that drink of sighs,
Or black collyrium for her weeping eyes?

Shatter her shining bracelets, break the string
Threading the mystic marriage-beads that cling
Loth to desert a sobbing throat so sweet,
Unbind the golden anklets on her feet,
Divest her of her azure veils and cloud
Her living beauty in a living shroud.

* * * * *

Nay, let her be! . . . what comfort can we give
For joy so frail, for hope so fugitive?
The yearning pain of unfulfilled delight,
The moonless vigils of her lonely night,
For the abysmal anguish of her tears,
And flowering springs that mock her empty years?

# AN INDIAN
# LOVE SONG

---

Written to an Indian tune

*He:*

LIFT up the veils that darken the delicate moon of thy
   glory and grace,
Withhold not, O Love, from the night of my longing the joy of
   thy luminous face,
Give me a spear of the scented *keora* guarding thy pinioned
   curls,
Or a silken thread from the fringes that trouble the dream of
   thy glimmering pearls;
Faint grows my soul with thy tresses' perfume and the song of
   thy anklets' caprice,
Revive me, I pray, with the magical nectar that dwells in the
   flower of thy kiss.

*She:*

How shall I yield to the voice of thy pleading, how shall I grant
    thy prayer,
Or give thee a rose-red silken tassel, a scented leaf from my
    hair?
Or fling in the flame of thy heart's desire the veils that cover my
    face.
Profane the law of my father's creed for a foe of my father's race?
Thy kinsmen have broken our sacred altars and slaughtered our
    sacred kine,
The feud of old faiths and the blood of old battles sever thy
    people and mine.

*He:*

What are the sins of my race, Beloved, what are my people to
    thee?
And what are thy shrine, and kine and kindred, what are thy
    gods to me?
Love recks not of feuds and bitter follies, of stranger, comrade
    or kin,
Alike in his ear sound the temple bells and the cry of the
    *muezzin.*
For Love shall cancel the ancient wrong and conquer the
    ancient rage,
Redeem with his tears the memoried sorrow that sullied a
    bygone age.

# IN REMEMBRANCE:

---

## VIOLET CLARKE

### Died March 21, 1909

WITH eager knowledge of our ancient lore,
And prescient love of all our ancient race,
You came to us, with gentle hands that bore
Bright gifts of genius, youth, and subtle grace,

Our shrines, our sacred streams, our sumptuous art,
Old hills that scale the sky's unageing dome,
Recalled some long-lost rapture to your heart,
Some far-off memory of your spirit's home.

* * * * *

We said: "She comes, an exquisite, strange flower
From the rich gardens of a northern king"...
But lo! our souls perceived you in that hour
The very rose whereof our poets sing.

Who sped your beauty's seed across the sea,
Bidding you burgeon in that alien clime?
And what prophetic wind of destiny
Restored you to us in your flowering time

For a brief season to delight and bless
Our hearts with delicate splendour and perfume,
Till Death usurped your vivid loveliness
In wanton envy of its radiant bloom?

O frail, miraculous flower, tho' you are dead,
The deathless fragrance of your spirit cleaves
To the dear wreath whereon our tears are shed,
Of your sweet wind-blown and love-garnered Leaves.[1]

---

1    "Leaves" is the title of her book of stories, published after
her death.

# LOVE AND DEATH

I DREAMED my love had set thy spirit free,
Enfranchised thee from Fate's o'ermastering power,
And girt thy being with a scatheless dower
Of rich and joyous immortality;
O Love, I dreamed my soul had ransomed thee,
In thy lone, dread, incalculable hour
From those pale hands at which all mortals cower,
And conquered Death by Love, like Savitri.
When I awoke, alas, my love was vain
E'en to annul one throe of destined pain,
Or by one heart-beat to prolong thy breath;
O Love, alas, that love could not assuage
The burden of thy human heritage,
Or save thee from the swift decrees of Death.

# THE DANCE OF LOVE

---

### Written for Madame Liza Lehmann

THE music sighs and slumbers,
It stirs and sleeps again . . .
Hush, it wakes and weeps and murmurs
Like a woman's heart in pain;
Now it laughs and calls and coaxes,
Like a lover in the night,
Now it pants with sudden longing,
Now it sobs with spent delight.

Like bright and wind-blown lilies,
The dancers sway and shine,
Swift in a rhythmic circle,
Soft in a rhythmic line;
Their lithe limbs gleam like amber
Thro' their veils of golden gauze,
As they glide and bend and beckon,
As they wheel and wind and pause.

The voices of lutes and cymbals
Fail on the failing breeze,
And the midnight's soul grows weary
With the scent of the champak trees;
But the subtle feet of the dancers
In a long, returning chain,
Wake in the heart of lovers
Love's ecstasy and pain.

# A LOVE SONG
# FROM THE NORTH

———————————

TELL me no more of thy love, *papeeha*,
Wouldst thou recall to my heart, *papeeha*,
Dreams of delight that are gone,
When swift to my side came the feet of my lover
With stars of the dusk and the dawn?
I see the soft wings of the clouds on the river,
And jewelled with raindrops the mango-leaves quiver,
And tender boughs flower on the plain. . . .
But what is their beauty to me, *papeeha*,
Beauty of blossom and shower, *papeeha*,
That brings not my lover again?

Tell me no more of thy love, *papeeha*,
Wouldst thou revive in my heart, *papeeha*,
Grief for the joy that is gone?
I hear the bright peacock in glimmering woodlands
Cry to its mate in the dawn;
I hear the black *koel's* slow, tremulous wooing,
And sweet in the gardens the calling and cooing
Of passionate bulbul and dove. . . .
But what is their music to me, *papeeha*,
Songs of their laughter and love, *papeeha*,
To me, forsaken of love?

The papeeha is a bird that comes in Northern India when the
mangoes are ripe, and calls "*Pi-kahan, Pi-kahan?*"—*Where is my
love?*

# AT TWILIGHT:

_____

## ON THE WAY TO GOLCONDA

WEARY, I sought kind Death among the rills
That drink of purple twilight where the plain
Broods in the shadow of untroubled hills:
I cried, "High dreams and hope and love are vain,
Absolve my spirit of its poignant ills,
And cleanse me from the bondage of my pain!

"Shall hope prevail where clamorous hate is rife,
Shall sweet love prosper or high dreams find place
Amid the tumult of reverberant strife
'Twixt ancient creeds, 'twixt race and ancient race,
That mars the grave, glad purposes of life,
Leaving no refuge save thy succouring face?"

\* \* \* \* \*

E'en as I spake, a mournful wind drew near,
Heavy with scent of drooping roses shed,
And incense scattered from the passing bier
Of some loved woman canopied in red,
Borne with slow chant and swift-remembering tear,
To the blind, ultimate silence of the dead. . .

O lost, O quenched in unawakening sleep
The glory of her dear, reluctant eyes!
O hushed the eager feet that knew the steep
And intricate ways of ecstasy and sighs!
And dumb with alien slumber, dim and deep,
The living heart that was love's paradise!

\* \* \* \* \*

Quick with the sense of joys she hath foregone,
Returned my soul to beckoning joys that wait,
Laughter of children and the lyric dawn,
And love's delight, profound and passionate,
Winged dreams that blow their golden clarion,
And hope that conquers immemorial hate.

# ALONE

---

ALONE, O Love, I seek the blossoming glades,
The bright, accustomed alleys of delight,
Pomegranate-gardens of the mellowing dawn,
Serene and sumptuous orchards of the night.

Alone, O Love, I breast the shimmering waves,
The changing tides of life's familiar streams,
Wide seas of hope, swift rivers of desire,
The moon-enchanted estuary of dreams.

But no compassionate wind or comforting star
Brings me sweet word of thine abiding place . . .
In what predestined hour of joy or tears
Shall I attain the sanctuary of thy face?

# A RAJPUT
# LOVE SONG

---

[PARVATI *at her lattice*]

O Love! were you a basil-wreath to twine among my tresses,
A jewelled clasp of shining gold to bind around my sleeve,
O Love! were you the *keora's* soul that haunts my silken
    raiment,
A bright, vermilion tassel in the girdles that I weave;

O Love! were you the scented fan that lies upon my pillow,
A sandal lute, or silver lamp that burns before my shrine,
Why should I fear the jealous dawn that spreads with cruel
    laughter,
Sad veils of separation between your face and mine?


*Haste, O wild-bee hours to the gardens of the sunset!*
*Fly, wild-parrot day to the orchards of the west!*
*Come, O tender night, with your sweet, consoling darkness,*
*And bring me my Beloved to the shelter of my breast!*

[AMAR SINGH *in the saddle*]

O Love! were you the hooded hawk upon my hand that flutters,
Its collar-band of gleaming bells atinkle as I ride,
O Love! were you a turban-spray or floating heron-feather,
The radiant, swift, unconquered sword that swingeth at my side;

O Love! were you a shield against the arrows of my foemen,
An amulet of jade against the perils of the way,
How should the drum-beats of the dawn divide me from your
    bosom,
Or the union of the midnight be ended with the day?


*Haste, O wild-deer hours, to the meadows of the sunset!*
*Fly, wild stallion day, to the pastures of the west!*
*Come O tranquil night, with your soft, consenting darkness,*
*And hear me to the fragrance of my 'Beloved's breast!*

# A PERSIAN LOVE SONG

O LOVE! I know not why, when you are glad,
Gaily my glad heart leaps.
Love! I know not why, when you are sad,
Wildly my sad heart weeps.

I know not why, if sweet be your repose,
My waking heart finds rest,
Or if your eyes be dim with pain, sharp throes
Of anguish rend my breast.

Hourly this subtle mystery flowers anew,
O Love, I know not why . . .
Unless it be, perchance, that I am you,
Dear love, that you are I!

# TO LOVE

O LOVE! of all the riches that are mine,
What gift have I withheld before thy shrine?

What tender ecstasy of prayer and praise
Or lyric flower of my impassioned days?

What poignant dream have I denied to thee
Of secret hope, desire and memory;

Or intimate anguish of sad years, long dead,
Old griefs unstaunched, old fears uncomforted?

What radiant prophecies that thrill and throng
The unborn years with swift delight of song?

O Love! of all the treasures that I own,
What gift have I withheld before thy throne?

# SONGS OF
# THE SPRINGTIME

## SPRING

---

YOUNG leaves grow green on the banyan twigs,
And red on the peepul tree,
The honey-birds pipe to the budding figs,
And honey-blooms call the bee.

Poppies squander their fragile gold
In the silvery aloe-brake,
Coral and ivory lilies unfold
Their delicate lives on the lake.

Kingfishers ruffle the feathery sedge,
And all the vivid air thrills
With butterfly-wings in the wild-rose hedge,
And the luminous blue of the hills.

Kamala tinkles a lingering foot
In the grove where temple-bells ring,
And Krishna plays on his bamboo flute
An idyl of love and spring.

# A SONG IN SPRING

WILD bees that rifle the mango blossom,
Set free awhile from the love-god's string,
Wild birds that sway in the citron branches,
Drunk with the rich, red honey of spring,

Fireflies weaving aërial dances
In fragile rhythms of flickering gold,
What do you know in your blithe, brief season
Of dreams deferred and a heart grown old?

But the wise winds know, as they pause to slacken
The speed of their subtle, omniscient flight,
Divining the magic of unblown lilies,
Foretelling the stars of the unborn night.

They have followed the hurrying feet of pilgrims,
Tracking swift prayers to their utmost goals,
They have spied on Love's old and changeless secret,
And the changing sorrow of human souls.

They have tarried with Death in her parleying-places,
And issued the word of her high decree,
Their wings have winnowed the garnered sunlight,
Their lips have tasted the purple sea.

# THE JOY OF
# THE SPRINGTIME

---

SPRINGTIME, O Springtime, what is your essence,
The lilt of a bulbul, the laugh of a rose,
The dance of the dew on the wings of a moonbeam,
The voice of the zephyr that sings as he goes,
The hope of a bride or the dream of a maiden
Watching the petals of gladness unclose?

Springtime, O Springtime, what is your secret,
The bliss at the core of your magical mirth,
That quickens the pulse of the morning to wonder
And hastens the seeds of all beauty to birth,
That captures the heavens and conquers to blossom
The roots of delight in the heart of the earth?

# VASANT PANCHAMI:

---

## LILAVATI'S LAMENT
## AT THE FEAST OF SPRING

Go, dragon-fly, fold up your purple wing,
Why will you bring me tidings of the spring?
O lilting *koels*, hush your rapturous notes,
O *dhadikulas*, still your passionate throats,
Or seek some further garden for your nest . . .
Your songs are poisoned arrows in my breast.

O quench your flame, ye crimson *gulmohors*,
That flaunt your dazzling bloom across my doors,
Furl your white bells, sweet *champa* buds that call
Wild bees to your ambrosial festival,
And hold your breath, O dear *sirisha* trees . . .
You slay my heart with bitter memories.

O joyous girls who rise at break of morn
With sandal-soil your thresholds to adorn,
Ye brides who streamward bear on jewelled feet
Your gifts of silver lamps and new-blown wheat,
I pray you dim your voices when you sing
Your radiant salutations to the spring.

*Hai!* what have I to do with nesting birds,
With lotus-honey, corn and ivory curds,
With plantain blossom and pomegranate fruit,
Or rose-wreathed lintels and rose-scented lute,

With lighted shrines and fragrant altar-fires
Where happy women breathe their hearts' desires?

For my sad life is doomed to be, alas,
Ruined and sere like sorrow-trodden grass,
My heart hath grown, plucked by the wind of grief,
Akin to fallen flower and faded leaf,
Akin to every lone and withered thing
That hath foregone the kisses of the spring.

*The Vasant Panchami* is the spring festival when Hindu girls and married women carry gifts of lighted lamps and new-grown corn as offerings to the goddess of the spring and set them afloat on the face of the waters. Hindu widows cannot take part in any festive ceremonials. Their portion is sorrow and austerity.

# IN A TIME OF FLOWERS

O LOVE! do you know the spring is here
With the lure of her magic flute? . . .
The old earth breaks into passionate bloom
At the kiss of her fleet, gay foot.
The burgeoning leaves on the almond boughs,
And the leaves on the blue wave's breast
Are crowned with the limpid and delicate light
Of the gems in your turban-crest.
The bright pomegranate buds unfold,
The frail wild lilies appear,
Like the blood-red jewels you used to fling
O'er the maidens that danced at the feast of spring
To welcome the new-born year.

O Love! do you know the spring is here? . . .
The dawn and the dusk grow rife
With scent and song and tremulous mirth,
The blind, rich travail of life.
The winds are drunk with the odorous breath
Of *henna*, *sarisha*, and *neem* . . .
Do they ruffle your cold, strange, tranquil sleep,
Or trouble your changeless dream
With poignant thoughts of the world you loved,
And the beauty you held so dear?
Do you long for a brief, glad hour to wake
From your lonely slumber for sweet love's sake,
To welcome the new-born year?

# IN PRAISE OF
# GULMOHUR BLOSSOMS

---

WHAT can rival your lovely hue
O gorgeous boon of the spring?
The glimmering red of a bridal robe,
Rich red of a wild bird's wing?
Or the mystic blaze of the gem that burns
On the brow of a serpent-king?

What can rival the valiant joy
Of your dazzling, fugitive sheen?
The limpid clouds of the lustrous dawn
That colour the ocean's mien?
Or the blood that poured from a thousand breasts
To succour a Rajput queen?[2]

What can rival the radiant pride
Of your frail, victorious fire?
The flame of hope or the flame of hate,
Quick flame of my heart's desire?
Or the rapturous light that leaps to heaven
From a true wife's funeral pyre?

---

2    Queen Padmini of Chitore, famous in Indian history and
song.

# NASTURTIUMS

---

POIGNANT and subtle and bitter perfume,
Exquisite, luminous, passionate bloom,
Your leaves interwoven of fragrance and fire
Are Savitri's sorrow and Sita's desire,
Draupadi's longing, Damayanti's fears,
And sweetest Sakuntala's magical tears.

These ore the immortal women of Sanscrit legend and song, whose poignant sorrows and radiant virtues still break the heart and inspire the lives of Indian women.

## GOLDEN CASSIA

O BRILLIANT blossoms that strew my way,
You are only woodland flowers they say.

But, I sometimes think that perchance you are
Fragments of some new-fallen star;

Or golden lamps for a fairy shrine,
Or golden pitchers for fairy wine.

Perchance you are, O frail and sweet!
Bright anklet-bells from the wild spring's feet,

Or the gleaming tears that some fair bride shed
Remembering her lost maidenhead.

But now, in the memoried dusk you seem
The glimmering ghosts of a bygone dream.

# CHAMPAK BLOSSOMS

AMBER petals, ivory petals,
Petals of carven jade,
Charming with your ambrosial sweetness
Forest and field and glade,
Foredoomed in your hour of transient glory
To shrivel and shrink and fade!

Tho' mango blossoms have long since vanished,
And orange blossoms be shed,
They live anew in the luscious harvests
Of ripening yellow and red;
But you, when your delicate bloom is over,
Will reckon amongst the dead.

Only to girdle a girl's dark tresses
Your fragrant hearts are uncurled:
Only to garland the vernal breezes
Your fragile stars are unfurled.
You make no boast in your purposeless beauty
To serve or profit the world.

Yet, 'tis of you thro' the moonlit ages
That maidens and minstrels sing,
And lay your buds on the great god's altar,
O radiant blossoms that fling
Your rich, voluptuous, magical perfume
To ravish the winds of spring.

## ECSTASY

————————

Heart, O my heart! lo, the springtime is waking
      In meadow and grove.
Lo, the mellifluous *koels* are making
      Their paeans of love.
Behold the bright rivers and rills in their glancing,
      Melodious flight,
Behold how the sumptuous peacocks are dancing
      In rhythmic delight.

Shall we in the midst of life's exquisite chorus
      Remember our grief,
O heart, when the rapturous season is o'er us
      Of blossom and leaf?
Their joy from the birds and the streams let us borrow,
      O heart! let us sing,
The years are before us for weeping and sorrow . . .
      *To-day* it is spring!

# INDIAN
# FOLK-SONGS
# TO INDIAN TUNES

## VILLAGE SONG

---

FULL are my pitchers and far to carry,
Lone is the way and long,
Why, O why was I tempted to tarry
Lured by the boatmen's song?
Swiftly the shadows of night are falling,
Hear, O hear, is the white crane calling,
Is it the wild owl's cry?
There are no tender moonbeams to light me,
If in the darkness a serpent should bite me,
Or if an evil spirit should smite me,
*Rām re Rām!* I shall die.

My brother will murmur "Why doth she linger?"
My mother will wait and weep,
Saying, "O safe may the great gods bring her,
The Jamuna's waters are deep." . . .
The Jamuna's waters rush by so quickly,
The shadows of evening gather so thickly,
Like black birds in the sky. . . .

O! if the storm breaks, what will betide me?
Safe from the lightning where shall I hide me?
Unless Thou succour my footsteps and guide me,
*Rām re Rām!* I shall die.

# SLUMBER
# SONG FOR SUNALINI

---

## In a Bengalee metre

WHERE the golden, glowing
Champak-buds are blowing,
By the swiftly-flowing streams,
Now, when day is dying,
There are fairies flying
Scattering a cloud of dreams.

Slumber-spirits winging
Thro' the forest singing,
Flutter hither bringing soon,
Baby-visions sheeny
For my Sunalini . . .
Hush thee, O my pretty moon!

Sweet, the saints shall bless thee . . .
Hush, mine arms caress thee,
Hush, my heart doth press thee, sleep,
Till the red dawn dances
Breaking thy soft trances,
Sleep, my Sunalini, sleep!

# SONGS OF MY CITY

----

## I.
## IN A LATTICED BALCONY

How shall I feed thee, Beloved?
*On golden-red honey and fruit.*
How shall I please thee, Beloved?
*With th' voice of the cymbal and lute.*

How shall I garland thy tresses?
*With pearls from the jessamine close.*
How shall I perfume thy fingers?
*With th' soul of the keora and rose.*

How shall I deck thee, O Dearest?
*In hues of the peacock and dove.*
How shall I woo thee, O Dearest?
*With the delicate silence of love.*

## II.
## IN THE BAZAARS OF HYDERABAD

*To a tune of the Bazaars*

WHAT do you sell, O ye merchants?
Richly your wares are displayed.
*Turbans of crimson and silver,*
*Tunics of purple brocade,*
*Mirrors with panels of amber,*
*Daggers with handles of jade.*

What do you weigh, O ye vendors?
*Saffron and lentil and rice.*
What do you grind, O ye maidens?
*Sandalwood, henna, and spice.*
What do you call, O ye pedlars?
*Chessmen and ivory dice.*

What do you make, O ye goldsmiths?
*Wristlet and anklet and ring,*
*Bells for the feet of blue pigeons,*
*Frail as a dragon-fly's wing,*
*Girdles of gold for the dancers,*
*Scabbards of gold for the king.*

What do you cry, O ye fruitmen?
*Citron, pomegranate, and plum.*
What do you play, O musicians?
*Cithār, sarangī, and drum.*
What do you chant, O magicians?
*Spells for the æons to come.*

What do you weave, O ye flower-girls
With tassels of azure and red?
*Crowns for the brow of a bridegroom,*
*Chaplets to garland his bed,*
*Sheets of white blossoms new-gathered*
*To perfume the sleep of the dead.*

# BANGLE-SELLERS

BANGLE-SELLERS are we who bear
Our shining loads to the temple fair. . . .
Who will buy these delicate, bright
Rainbow-tinted circles of light?
Lustrous tokens of radiant lives,
For happy daughters and happy wives.

Some are meet for a maiden's wrist,
Silver and blue as the mountain-mist,
Some are flushed like the buds that dream
On the tranquil brow of a woodland stream;
Some are aglow with the bloom that cleaves
To the limpid glory of new-born leaves.

Some are like fields of sunlit corn,
Meet for a bride on her bridal morn,
Some, like the flame of her marriage fire,
Or rich with the hue of her heart's desire,
Tinkling, luminous, tender, and clear,
Like her bridal laughter and bridal tear.

Some are purple and gold-flecked grey,
For her who has journeyed thro' life midway,
Whose hands have cherished, whose love has blest
And cradled fair sons on her faithful breast,
Who serves her household in fruitful pride,
And worships the gods at her husband's side.

# THE
# FESTIVAL OF SERPENTS

---

SHINING ones awake, we seek your chosen temples
In caves and sheltering sandhills and sacred banyan roots;
O lift your dreaming heads from their trance of ageless wisdom,
And weave your mystic measures to the melody of flutes.

We bring you milk and maize, wild figs and golden honey,
And kindle fragrant incense to hallow all the air,
With fasting lips we pray, with fervent hearts we praise you,
O bless our lowly offerings and hearken to our prayer.

Guard our helpless lives and guide our patient labours,
And cherish our dear vision like the jewels in your crests;
O spread your hooded watch for the safety of our slumbers,
And soothe the troubled longings that clamour in our breasts.

Swift are ye as streams and soundless as the dewfall,
Subtle as the lightning and splendid as the sun;
Seers are ye and symbols of the ancient silence,
Where life and death and sorrow and ecstasy are one.

# SONG OF
# RADHA THE MILKMAID

I CARRIED my curds to the Mathura fair. . . .
How softly the heifers were lowing. . . .
I wanted to cry "Who will buy, who will buy
These curds that are white as the clouds in the sky
When the breezes of *Shrawan* are blowing?"
But my heart was so full of your beauty, Beloved,
They laughed as I cried without knowing:
      *Govinda! Govinda!*
      *Govinda! Govinda!* . . .
How softly the river was flowing!

I carried my pots to the Mathura tide. . . .
How gaily the rowers were rowing! . . .
My comrades called "Ho! let us dance, let us sing
And wear saffron garments to welcome the spring,
And pluck the new buds that are blowing."
But my heart was so full of your music, Beloved,
They mocked when I cried without knowing:
      *Govinda! Govinda!*
      *Govinda! Govinda!* . . .
How gaily the river was flowing!

I carried my gifts to the Mathura shrine. . . .
How brightly the torches were glowing! . . .
I folded my hands at the altars to pray
"O shining Ones guard us by night and by day"—
And loudly the conch shells were blowing.
But my heart was so lost in your worship, Beloved,
They were wroth when I cried without knowing:
*Govinda! Govinda!*
*Govinda! Govinda!* . . .
How brightly the river was flowing!

Mathura is the chief centre of the mystic worship of Khrishna, the Divine Cowherd and Musician—the "Divine Beloved" of every Hindu heart. He is also called Govinda.

# SPINNING SONG

PAMDINI:

My sisters plucked green leaves at morn
To deck the garden swing,
And donned their shining golden veils
For the Festival of Spring. . . .
But sweeter than the new-blown vines,
And the call of nesting birds
Are the tendrils of your hair, Beloved,
And the music of your words.

MAYURA:

My sisters sat beside the hearth
Kneading the saffron cakes,
They gathered honey from the hives
For the Festival of Snakes. . . .
Why should I wake the jewelled lords
With offerings or vows,
Who wear the glory of your love
Like a jewel on my brows?

SARASVATI:

My sisters sang at evenfall
A hymn of ancient rites,
And kindled rows of silver lamps
For the Festival of Lights. . . .
But I leaned against the lattice-door
To watch the kindling skies,
And praised the gracious gods, Beloved,
For the beauty of your eyes.

The Festivals are known respectively as the *Vasant Panchami, Nagpanchami*, and *Depavali.*

# HYMN TO INDRA, LORD OF RAIN

*Men's Voices:*

O THOU, who rousest the voice of the thunder,
And biddest the storms to awake from their sleep,
Who breakest the strength of the mountains asunder,
And cleavest the manifold pride of the deep!
Thou, who with bountiful torrent and river
Dost nourish the heart of the forest and plain,
Withhold not Thy gifts O Omnipotent Giver!
        Hearken, O Lord of Rain!

*Women's Voices:*

O Thou, who wieldest Thy deathless dominion
O'er mutable legions of earth and the sky,
Who grantest the eagle the joy of her pinion,
And teachest the young of the *koel* to fly!
Thou who art mighty to succour and cherish,
Who savest from sorrow and shieldest from pain,
Withhold not Thy merciful love, or we perish,
        Hearken, O Lord of Rain!

# SONGS OF LIFE

## DEATH AND LIFE

----

DEATH stroked my hair and whispered tenderly:
"Poor child, shall I redeem thee from thy pain,
Renew thy joy and issue thee again
Inclosed in some renascent ecstasy . . .
Some lilting bird or lotus-loving bee,
Or the diaphanous silver of the rain,
Th' alluring scent of the sirisha-plain,
The wild wind's voice, the white wave's melody?"

I said, "Thy gentle pity shames mine ear,
O Death, am I so purposeless a thing,
Shall my soul falter or my body fear
Its poignant hour of bitter suffering,
Or fail ere I achieve my destined deed
Of song or service for my country's need?"

# THE HUSSAIN SAAGAR

THE young dawn woos thee with his amorous grace,
The journeying clouds of sunset pause and hover,
Drinking the beauty of thy luminous face,
But none thine inmost glory may discover,
For thine evasive silver doth enclose
What secret purple and what subtle rose
Responsive only to the wind, thy lover.
Only for him thy shining waves unfold
Translucent music answering his control;
Thou dost, like me, to one allegiance hold,
O lake, O living image of my soul.

# THE FAERY
# ISLE OF JANJIRA

———————

### To Her Highness Nazli Raffia,
### Begum of Janjira

FAIN would I dwell in your faery kingdom,
O faery queen of a flowering clime,
Where life glides by to a delicate measure,
With the glamour and grace of a far-off time.

Fain would I dwell where your wild doves wander,
Your palm-woods burgeon and sea-winds sing. . . .
Lulled by the rune of the rhythmic waters,
In your Island of Bliss it is always spring.

Yet must I go where the loud world beckons,
And the urgent drum-beat of destiny calls,
Far from your white dome's luminous slumber,
Far from the dream of your fortress walls,

Into the strife of the throng and the tumult,
The war of sweet Love against folly and wrong;
Where brave hearts carry the sword of battle,
'Tis mine to carry the banner of song,

The solace of faith to the lips that falter,
The succour of hope to the hands that fail,
The tidings of joy when Peace shall triumph,
When Truth shall conquer and Love prevail.

119

# THE SOUL'S PRAYER

---

In childhood's pride I said to Thee:
"O Thou, who mad'st me of Thy breath,
Speak, Master, and reveal to me
Thine inmost laws of life and death.

"Give me to drink each joy and pain
Which Thine eternal hand can mete,
For my insatiate soul would drain
Earth's utmost bitter, utmost sweet.

"Spare me no bliss, no pang of strife,
Withhold no gift or grief I crave,
The intricate lore of love and life
And mystic knowledge of the grave."

Lord, Thou didst answer stern and low:
"Child, I will hearken to thy prayer,
And thy unconquered soul shall know
All passionate rapture and despair.

"Thou shalt drink deep of joy and fame,
And love shall burn thee like a fire,
And pain shall cleanse thee like a flame,
To purge the dross from thy desire.

"So shall thy chastened spirit yearn
To seek from its blind prayer release,
And spent and pardoned, sue to learn
The simple secret of My peace

"I, bending from my sevenfold height
Will teach thee of My quickening grace,
*Life is a prism of My light,*
*And Death the shadow of My face."*

# TRANSIENCE

NAY, do not grieve tho' life be full of sadness,
Dawn will not veil her splendour for your grief,
Nor spring deny their bright, appointed beauty
To lotus blossom and ashoka leaf.

Nay, do not pine, tho' life be dark with trouble,
Time will not pause or tarry on his way;
To-day that seems so long, so strange, so bitter,
Will soon be some forgotten yesterday.

Nay, do not weep; new hopes, new dreams, new faces,
The unspent joy of all the unborn years,
Will prove your heart a traitor to its sorrow,
And make your eyes unfaithful to their tears.

# THE OLD WOMAN

A LONELY old woman sits out in the street
'Neath the boughs of a banyan tree,
And hears the bright echo of hurrying feet,
The pageant of life going blithely and fleet
   To the feast of eternity.

Her tremulous hand holds a battered white bowl,
If perchance in your pity you fling her a dole;
She is poor, she is bent, she is blind,
But she lifts a brave heart to the jest of the days,
And her withered, brave voice croons its paean of praise,
Be the gay world kind or unkind:
   *"La ilaha illa-l-Allah,*
   *La ilaha illa-l-Allah,*
   *Muhammad-ar-Rasul-Allah."*

In hope of your succour, how often in vain,
So patient she sits at my gates,
In the face of the sun and the wind and the rain,
Holding converse with poverty, hunger and pain,
And the ultimate sleep that awaits. . . .
In her youth she hath comforted lover and son,
In her weary old age, O dear God, is there none
To bless her tired eyelids to rest? . . .
Tho' the world may not tarry to help her or heed,
More clear than the cry of her sorrow and need
Is the faith that doth solace her breast:
   *"La ilaha illa-l-Allah,*
   *La ilaha illa-l-Allah,*
   *Muhammad-ar-Rasul-Allah."*

# IN THE NIGHT

---

SLEEP, O my little ones, sleep,
Safe till the daylight be breaking . . .
We have long vigils to keep,
Harvests to sow while you sleep,
Fair for the hour of your waking,
Ripe for your sickles to reap.

Sleep, O my little ones, sleep,
Yours is the golden To-morrow,
Yours are the hands that will reap
Dreams that we sow while you sleep,
Fed with our hope and our sorrow,
Rich with the tears that we weep.

# AT DAWN

CHILDREN, my children, the daylight is breaking,
The cymbals of morn sound the hour of your waking,
The long night is o'er, and our labour is ended,
Fair blow the fields that we tilled and we tended,
Swiftly the harvest grows mellow for reaping,
The harvest we sowed in the time of your sleeping.

Weak were our hands but our service was tender,
In darkness we dreamed of the dawn of your splendour,
In silence we strove for the joy of the morrow,
And watered your seeds from the wells of our sorrow,
We toiled to enrich the glad hour of your waking,
Our vigil is done, lo ! the daylight is breaking.

Children, my children, who wake to inherit
The ultimate hope of our travailing spirit,
Say, when your young hearts shall take to their keeping
The manifold dreams we have sown for your reaping,
Is it praise, is it pain you will grant us for guerdon?
Anoint with your love or arraign with your pardon?

# AN ANTHEM OF LOVE

Two hands are we to serve thee, O our Mother,
To strive and succour, cherish and unite;
Two feet are we to cleave the waning darkness,
And gain the pathways of the dawning light.

Two ears are we to catch the nearing echo,
The sounding cheer of Time's prophetic horn;
Two eyes are we to reap the crescent glory,
The radiant promise of renascent morn.

One heart are we to love thee, O our Mother,
One undivided, indivisible soul,
Bound by one hope, one purpose, one devotion
Towards a great, divinely-destined goal.

## SOLITUDE

LET us rise, O my heart, let us go where the twilight is calling
Far away from the sound of this lonely and menacing crowd,
To the glens, to the glades, where the magical darkness is falling
In rivers of gold from the breast of a radiant cloud.

Come away, come away from this throng and its tumult of
    sorrow,
There is rest, there is peace from the pang of its manifold strife
Where the halcyon night holds in trust the dear songs of the
    morrow,
And the silence is but a rich pause in the music of life.

Let us climb where the eagles keep guard on the rocky grey
    ledges,
Let us lie 'neath the palms where perchance we may listen, and
    reach
A delicate dream from the lips of the slumbering sedges,
That catch from the stars some high tone of their mystical
    speech.

Or perchance, we may glean a far glimpse of the Infinite Bosom
In whose glorious shadow all life is unfolded or furled.
Thro' the luminous hours ere the lotus of dawn shall reblossom
In petals of splendour to worship the Lord of the world.

# A CHALLENGE TO FATE

WHY will you vex me with your futile conflict,
Why will you strive with me, O foolish Fate?
You cannot break me with your poignant envy,
You cannot slay me with your subtle hate:
For all the cruel folly you pursue
I will not cry with suppliant hands to you.

You may perchance wreck in your bitter malice
The radiant empire of mine eager eyes . . .
Say, can you rob my memory's dear dominion
O'er sunlit mountains and sidereal skies?
In my enduring treasuries I hold
Their ageless splendour of unravished gold.

You may usurp the kingdoms of my hearing . . .
Say, shall my scatheless spirit cease to hear
The bridal rapture of the blowing valleys,
The lyric pageant of the passing year,
The sounding odes and surging harmonies
Of battling tempests and unconquered seas?

Yea, you may smite my mouth to throbbing silence,
Pluck from my lips power of articulate words . . .
Say, shall my heart lack its familiar language
While earth has nests for her mellifluous birds?
Shall my impassioned heart forget to sing
With the ten thousand voices of the spring?

Yea, you may quell my blood with sudden anguish,
Fetter my limbs with some compelling pain . . .
How will you daunt my free, far-journeying fancy
That rides upon the pinions of the rain?
How will you tether my triumphant mind,
Rival and fearless comrade of the wind?

\* \* \* \* \*

Tho' you deny the hope of all my being,
Betray my love, my sweetest dream destroy,
Yet will I slake my individual sorrow
At the deep source of Universal joy. . . .
O Fate, in vain you hanker to control
My frail, serene, indomitable soul.

129

# THE CALL
# TO EVENING PRAYER

———————————

*Allah ho Akbar! Allah ho Akbar!*
From mosque and minar the muezzins are calling;
Pour forth your praises, O Chosen of Islam;
Swiftly the shadows of sunset are falling:
*Allah ho Akbar! Allah ho Akbar!*

*Ave Maria! Ave Maria!*
Devoutly the priests at the altars are singing;
O ye who worship the Son of the Virgin,
Make your orisons, the vespers are ringing:
*Ave Maria! Ave Maria!*

*Ahura Mazda! Ahura Mazda!*
How the sonorous Avesta is flowing!
Ye, who to Flame and the light make obeisance,
Bend low where the quenchless blue torches are glowing:

*Ahura Mazda! Ahura Mazda!*
*Naray'yana! Naray'yana!*
Hark to the ageless, divine invocation!
Lift up your hands, O ye children of Bramha,
Lift up your voices in rapt adoration:
*Naray'yana! Naray'yana!*

# IN SALUTATION
# TO THE ETERNAL PEACE

MEN say the world is full of fear and hate,
And all life's ripening harvest-fields await
The restless sickle of relentless fate.

But I, sweet Soul, rejoice that I was born,
When from the climbing terraces of corn
I watch the golden orioles of Thy morn.

What care I for the world's desire and pride,
Who know the silver wings that gleam and glide,
The homing pigeons of Thine eventide?

What care I for the world's loud weariness,
Who dream in twilight granaries Thou dost bless
With delicate sheaves of mellow silences?

Say, shall I heed dull presages of doom,
Or dread the rumoured loneliness and gloom,
The mute and mythic terror of the tomb?

For my glad heart is drunk and drenched with Thee,
O inmost wine of living ecstasy!
O intimate essence of eternity!

## MEDLEY

―――――――――

### A Kashmeri Song

THE poppy grows on the roof-top,
The iris flowers on the grave;
Hope in the heart of a lover,
And fear in the heart of a slave.

The opal lies in the river,
The pearl in the ocean's breast;
Doubt in a grieving bosom,
And faith in a heart at rest.

Fireflies dance in the moon-light,
Peach-leaves dance in the wind;
Dreams and delicate fancies
Dance thro' a poet's mind.

Sweetness dwells in the beehive,
And lives in a maiden's breath;
Joy in the eyes of children
And peace in the hands of Death.

# FAREWELL

BRIGHT shower of lambent butterflies,
Soft cloud of murmuring bees,
O fragile storm of sighing leaves
Adrift upon the breeze!

Wild birds with eager wings outspread
To seek an alien sky,
Sweet comrades of a lyric spring.
My little songs, good-bye !

# GUERDON

To field and forest
The gifts of the spring,
To hawk and to heron
The pride of their wing;
Her grace to the panther,
Her tints to the dove. . .
For me, O my Master,
The rapture of Love!

To the hand of the diver
The gems of the tide,
To the eyes of the bridegroom
The face of his bride;

To the heart of a dreamer
The dreams of his youth. . .
For me, O my Master,
The rapture of Truth!

To priests and to prophets
The joy of their creeds,
To kings and their cohorts
The glory of deeds;
And peace to the vanquished
And hope to the strong. . . .
For me, O my Master,
The rapture of Song!

# THE
# BROKEN WING

# SONGS OF
# LIFE AND DEATH

## THE BROKEN WING

_____

### *QUESTION*

THE great dawn breaks, the mournful night is past,
From her deep age-long sleep she wakes at last!
Sweet and long-slumbering buds of gladness ope
Fresh lips to the returning winds of hope,
Our eager hearts renew their radiant flight
Towards the glory renascent light,
Life and our land await their destined spring
Song-bird why dost thou bear a broken wing?

## *ANSWER*

Shall spring that wakes mine ancient land again
Call to my wild and suffering heart in vain?
Or Fate's blind arrows still the pulsing note
Of my far-reaching, frail, unconquered throat?
Or a weak bleeding pinion daunt or tire
My flight to the high realms of my desire?
Behold! I rise to meet the destined spring
And scale the stars upon my broken wing!

# THE GIFT OF INDIA

Is there aught you need that my hands withhold,
Rich gifts of raiment or grain or gold?
Lo! I have flung to the East and West
Priceless treasures torn from my breast,
And yielded the sons of my stricken womb
To the drum-beats of duty, the sabres of doom.

Gathered like pearls in their alien gravès
Silent they sleep by the Persian waves,
Scattered like shells on Egyptian sands,
They lie with pale brows and brave, broken hands,
They are strewn like blossoms mown down by chance
On the blood-brown meadows of Flanders and France.

Can ye measure the grief of the tears I weep
Or compass the woe of the watch I keep?
Or the pride that thrills thro' my heart's despair
And the hope that comforts the anguish of prayer?
And the far sad glorious vision I see
Of the torn red banners of Victory?

When the terror and tumult of hate shall cease
And life be refashioned on anvils of peace,
And your love shall offer memorial thanks
To the comrades who fought in your dauntless ranks,
And you honour the deeds of the deathless ones,
Remember the blood of my martyred sons!

*August* 1915

# THE TEMPLE

---

### Priest

AWAKE, it is Love's radiant hour of praise!
Bring new-blown leaves his temple to adorn,
Pomegranate-buds and ripe sirisha -sprays,
Wet sheaves of shining corn.

### Pilgrim

*O priest! only my broken lute I bring*
*For Love's praise-offering!*

### Priest

Behold! the hour of sacrifice draws near.
Pile high the gleaming altar-stones of Love
With delicate burdens of slain woodland deer
And frail white mountain dove.

### Pilgrim

*O priest! only my wounded heart I bring*
*For Love's blood-offering!*

### Priest

Lo! now it strikes Lover's solemn hour of prayer,
Kindle with fragrant boughs his blazing shrine,
Feed the sweet flame with spice and incense rare,
Curds of rose-pastured kine.

### Pilgrim

*O priest! only my stricken soul I bring*
*For Love's burnt-offering!*

# LAKSHMI,
# THE LOTUS-BORN

---

### Goddess of Fortune

THOUGH who didst rise like a pearl from the ocean,
Whose beauty surpasseth the splendour of morn!
Lo! We invoke thee with eager devotion,
      Hearken, O Lotus-born!

Come! With sweet eyelids and fingers caressing,
With footfalls auspicious our thresholds adorn,
And grant us the showers and the sheaves of thyblessing,
      Hearken, O Lotus-born!

Prosper our cradles and kindred and cattle,
And cherish our hearth-fires and coffers and corn,
O watch o'er our seasons of peace and of battle,
      Hearken, O Lotus-born!

For our dear Land do we offer oblation,
O keep thou her glory unsullied, unshorn,
And guard the invincible hope of our nation,
      Hearken, O Lotus-born!

*Lakshmi Puja Day,* 1915

# THE VICTOR

THEY brought their peacock-lutes of praise
And carven gems in jasper trays,
Rich stores of fragrant musk and myrrh,
And wreaths of scarlet nenuphar . . .
I had no offering that was meet,
And bowed my face upon his feet.

They brought him robes from regal looms,
Inwrought with pearl and silver blooms,
And sumptuous footcloths broideréd
With beetle-wings and gleaming thread . . .
I had no offering that was meet,
And spread my hands beneath his feet.

They filled his courts with gifts of price,
With tiers of grain and towers of spice,
Tall jars of golden oil and wine,
And heads of camel and of kine . . .
I had no offering that was meet,
And laid my life before his feet.

# THE IMAM BARA

Of Lucknow

## I

OUT of the sombre shadows,
Over the sunlit grass,
Slow in a sad procession
The shadowy pageants pass
Mournful, majestic, and solemn,
Stricken and pale and dumb,
Crowned in their peerless anguish
The sacred martyrs come.
Hark, from the brooding silence
Breaks the wild cry of pain
Wrung from the heart of the ages
  *Ali! Hassan! Hussain!*

## II

COME from this tomb of shadows,
Come from this tragic shrine
That throbs with the deathless sorrow
Of a long-dead martyr line.
Love! let the living sunlight
Kindle your splendid eyes
Ablaze with the steadfast triumph
Of the spirit that never dies.
So may the hope of new ages
Comfort the mystic pain
That cries from the ancient silence
    *Ali! Hassan! Hussain!*

The Imam Bara is a Chapel of Lamentation where Mussulmans of the Shiah Community celebrate the tragic martyrdom of Ali, Hassan, and Hussain, during the mourning month of Moharram. A sort of passion-play takes place to the accompaniment of the refrain, Ali! Hassan! Hussain!

# A SONG FROM SHIRAZ

THE singers of Shiraz are feasting afar
To greet the Nauraz with sarang and cithar . . .
But what is their music that calleth to me,
From glimmering garden and glowing minar?

*The stars shall be scattered like jewels of glass,*
*And Beauty be tossed like a shell in the sea,*
*Ere the lutes of their magical laughter surpass*
*The lute, of thy tears, O Mohamed Ali!*

From the Mosque-towers of Shiraz ere daylight begin
My heart is disturbed by the loud muezzin,
But what is the voice of his warning to me,
That waketh the world to atonement of sin?

*The stars shall be broken like mirrors of brass,*
*And Rapture be sunk like a stone in the sea,*
*Ere the carpet of prayer or of penance surpass*
*Thy carpet of dreams, O Mohamed Ali!*

In the silence of Shiraz my soul shall await,
Untroubled, the wandering Angel of Fate
What terror or joy shall his hands hold for me,
Who bringeth the goblet of guerdon too late?

*The stars shall be mown and uprooted like grass,*
*And Glory be flung like a weed in the sea,*
*Ere the goblet of doom or salvation surpass*
*Thy goblet of love, O Mohamed Ali!*

146

# IMPERIAL DELHI

IMPERIAL CITY! dowered with sovereign grace,
To thy renascent glory still there clings
The splendid tragedy of ancient things,
The regal woes of many a vanquished race;
And memory's tears are cold upon thy face
E'en while thy heart's returning gladness rings
Loud on the sleep of thy forgotten Kings,
Who in thine arms sought Life's last resting-place.

Thy changing Kings and Kingdoms pass away,
The gorgeous legends of a bygone day,
But thou dost still immutably remain
Unbroken symbol of proud histories,
Unageing priestess of old mysteries
Before whose shrine the spells of Death are vain.

1912

# MEMORIAL VERSES

## I.

_____

### YA MAHBUB!

ARE these the streets that I used to know —
Was it yesterday or aeons ago?
Where are the armies that used to wait —
The pilgrims of Love — at your palace gate?
The joyous paeans that thrilled the air
The pageants that shone thro' your palace square?
And the minstrel music that used to ring
Thro' your magic kingdom . . . when you were king?

O hands that succoured a people's need
With the splendour of Haroun-al-Rasheed!
O heart that solaced a sad world's cry
With the sumptuous bounty of Hatim tai!
Where are the days that were winged and clad
In the fabulous glamour of old Baghdad.

And the bird of glory used to sing
In your magic kingdom ... when you were king?

O king, in your kingdom there is no change.
'Tis only my soul that hath grown so strange,
So faint with sorrow it cannot hear
Aught save the chant at your rose-crowned bier.
My grieving bosom hath grown too cold
To clasp the beauty it treasured of old,
The grace of life and the gifts of spring,
And the dreams I cherished ... when you were king!

*August* 29, 1911

"Ya Mahbub," which means O Beloved, was the device on the
State banner of the late Nizam of Hyderabad, Mir Mahbub Ali
Khan, the well-beloved of his people.

# II.

---

## GOKHALE

HEROIC Heart! lost hope of all our days!
Need'st thou the homage of our love or praise?
Lo! let the mournful millions round thy pyre
Kindle their souls with consecrated fire
Caught from the brave torch fallen from thy hand,
To succour and to serve our suffering land,
And in a daily worship taught by thee.
Upbuild the temple of her Unity.

*February* 19, 1915

Gopal Krishna Gokhale, the great saint and soldier of our national righteousness. His life was a sacrament, and his death was a sacrifice in the cause of Indian unity.

# III.

---

## IN THE SALUTATION
## TO MY FATHER'S SPIRIT

### Aghoremath Chattopadhyay

FAREWELL, Farewell, O brave and tender Sage.
O mystic jester, golden-hearted Child!
Selfless, serene, untroubled, unbeguiled
By trivial snares of grief and greed or rage;
O splendid dreamer in a dreamless age
Whose deep alchemic vision reconciled
Time's changing message with the undefiled
Calm wisdom of thy Vedic heritage!

Farewell, great spirit, without fear or flaw,
Thy life was love and liberty thy law,
And truth thy pure imperishable goal . . .
All hail to thee in thy transcendant flight
From hope to hope, from height to heav'nlier height,
Lost in the rapture of the Cosmic Soul.

*January* 28, 1915

# THE
# FLUTE-PLAYER
# OF BRINDABAN

WHY didst thou play thy matchless flute
   'Neath the Kadamba tree,
And wound my idly dreaming heart
   With poignant melody,
So where thou goest I must go
   My flute-player with thee?

Still must I like a homeless bird
   Wander, forsaking all
The earthly loves and worldly lures
   That held my life in thrall,
'And follow, follow, answering
   Thy magical flute-call.

To Indra's golden-flowering groves
   Where streams immortal flow,
Or to sad Yama's silent Courts
   Engulfed in lampless woe,
Where'er thy subtle flute I hear
   Belovèd I must go!

No peril of the deep or height
   Shall daunt my wingèd foot;
No fear of time-unconquered space,
   Or light untravelled route,
Impede my heart that pants to drain
   The nectar of thy flute!

Krishna, the Divine Flute-player of Brindaban, who plays the tune of the infinite that lures every Hindu heart away from mortal cares and attachments.

# FAREWELL

FAREWELL, O eager faces that surround me,
Claiming the tender service of my days,
Farewell, O joyous spirits that have bound me
With the love-sprinkled garlands of your praise!

O golden lamps of hope, how shall I bring you
Life's kindling flame from a forsaken fire?
O glowing hearts of youth, how shall I sing you
Life's glorious message from a broken lyre?

To you what further homage shall I render,
Victorious City girdled by the sea,
Where breaks in surging tides of woe and splendour
The age-long tumult of Humanity?

Need you another tribute for a token
Who reft from me the pride of all my years?
Lo! I will leave you with farewell unspoken,
Shrine of dead dream! O temple of my tears!

# THE CHALLENGE

---

THOU who dost quell in thy victorious tide
Death's ravaged secret and life's ruined pride,
Shall thy great deeps prevail, O conquering Sea,
O'er Love's relentless tides of memory?

Sweet Earth, though in thy lustrous bowl doth shine
The limpid flame of hope's perennial wine,
Thou art too narrow and too frail to bear
The harsh, wild vintage of my heart's despair.

O valiant skies, so eager to uphold
High laughing burdens of sidereal gold,
Swift would your brave brows perish to sustain
The radiant silence of my sleepless pain.

# WANDERING BEGGARS

FROM the threshold of the Dawn
On we wander, always on
Till the friendly light be gone
    *Y' Allah! Y' Allah!*

We are free-born sons of Fate,
What care we for wealth or state
Or the glory of the great?
    *Y' Allah! Y' Allah!*

Life may grant us or withhold
Roof or raiment, bread or gold,
But our hearts are gay and bold.
    *Y' Allah! Y' Allah!*

Time is like a wind that blows,
The future is a folded rose,
Who shall pluck it no man knows,
    *Y' Allah! Y' Allah!*

So we go a fearless band,
The staff of freedom in our hand
Wandering from land to land,
    *Y' Allah! Y' Allah!*

Till we meet the Night that brings
Both to beggars and to kings
The end of all their journeyings,
    *Y' Allah! Y' Allah!*

# THE LOTUS

To M. K. Gandhi

O MYSTIC Lotus, sacred and sublime,
　In myriad-petalled grace inviolate,
　Supreme o'er transient storms of tragic Fate,
　Deep-rooted in the waters of all Time,
　What legions loosed from many a far-off clime
　Of wild-bee hordes with lips insatiate,
　And hungry winds with wings of hope or hate,
　Have thronged and pressed round thy miraculous prime
　To devastate thy loveliness, to drain
　The midmost rapture of thy glorious heart . . .
　But who could win thy secret, who attain
　Thine ageless beauty born of Brahma's breath,
　Or pluck thine immortality, who art
　Coeval with the Lords of Life and Death?

# THE PRAYER OF ISLAM

---

WE praise Thee, O Compassionate!
Master of Life and Time and Fate,
Lord of the labouring winds and seas,
*Ya Hameed! Ya Hafeez!*

Thou art the Radiance of our ways,
Thou art the Pardon of our days,
Whose name is known from star to star,
*Ya Ghani! Ya Ghaffar!*

Thou art the Goal for which we long,
Thou art our Silence and our Song,
Life of the sunbeam and the seed —
*Ya Wahab! Ya Waheed!*

Thou dost transmute from hour to hour
Our mortal weakness into power
Our bondage into liberty,
*Ya Quadeer! Ya Quavi!*

We are the shadows of Thy light,
We are the secrets of Thy might,
The visions of thy primal dream,
*Ya Rahman! Ya Raheem!* [3]

*Id-uz-Zoha*, 1915

---

3    These are some of the Ninety-nine beautiful Arabic Names
of God as used by followers of Islam.

# BELLS

---

### Anklet-bells

ANKLET-BELLS! frail anklet-bells!
That hold Love's ancient mystery
As hide the lips of limpid shells
Faint tones of the remembered sea,
You murmur of enchanted rites,
Of sobbing breath and broken speech,
Sweet anguish of rose-scented nights
And wild mouths calling each to each
Or mute with yearning ecstasy.

### Cattle-bells

Cattle-bells! soft cattle-bells!
What gracious memories you bring
Of drowsy fields and dreaming wells,
And weary labour's folded wing,
Of frugal mirth round festal fires,
Brief trysts that youth and beauty keep,
Of flowering roofs and fragrant byres
White heifers gathered in for sleep,
Old songs the wandering women sing.

## Temple-bells

Temple-bells! deep temple-bells!
Whose urgent voices wreck the sky!
In your importance music dwells
Man's sad and immemorial cry
That cleaves the dawn with wings of praise,
That cleaves the dark with wings of prayer,
Craves pity for our mortal ways,
Seeks solace for our life's despair,
And peace for suffering hearts that die!

# THE
# GARDEN VIGIL

---

In the deep silence of the garden-bowers
Only the stealthy zephyr glides and goes,
Rifling the secret of sirisha flowers,
And to the new-born hours
Bequeathes the subtle anguish of the rose.

Pain-weary and dream-worn I lie awake,
Counting like beads the blazing stars o'erhead;
Round me the wind-stirred champak branches shake
Blossoms that fall and break
In perfumed rain across my lonely bed.

Long ere the sun's first far-off beacons shine,
Or her prophetic clarions call afar,
The gorgeous planets wither and decline,
Save in its eastern shrine,
Unquenched, unchallenged, the proud morning star.

O glorious light of hope beyond all reach!
O lovely symbol and sweet sign of him
Whose voice I yearn to hear in tender speech
To comfort me or teach,
Before whose gaze thy golden fires grow dim!

I care not what brave splendours bloom or die
So thou dost burn in thine appointed place,
Supreme in the still dawn-uncoloured sky,
And daily grant that I
May in thy flame adore His hidden face.

# INVINCIBLE

O FATE, betwixt the grinding-stones of Pain,
Tho' you have crushed my life like broken grain,
Lo! I will leaven it with my tears and knead
The bread of Hope to comfort and to feed
The myriad hearts for whom no harvests blow
    Save bitter herbs of woe.

Tho' in the flame of sorrow you have thrust
My flowering soul and trod it into dust,
Behold, it doth reblossom like a grove
To shelter under quickening boughs of Love
The myriad souls for whom no gardens bloom
    Save bitter buds of doom.

# THE PEARL

How long shall it suffice
    Merely to hoard in thine unequalled rays
   The bright sequestered colours of the sun,
O pearl above all price,
    And beautiful beyond all need of praise,
   World-coveted but yet possessed of none,
   Content in thy proud self-dominion?

Shall not some ultimate
    And unknown hour deliver thee, an attest
   Life's urgent and inviolable claim
To bind and consecrate
    The glory on some pure and bridal breast,
   Or set thee to enhance with flawless flame
   A new-born nation's coronal of fame?

Or wilt thou self-denied
    Forgo such sweet and sacramental ties
   As weld Love's delicate bonds of ecstasy,
And in a barren pride
    Of cold, unfruitful freedom that belies
   The inmost secret of fine liberty
   Return unblest into the primal sea?

# THREE SORROWS

How shall I honour thee, O sacred grief?
Fain would my love transmute
My suffering into music and my heart
Into a deathless lute!

How shall I cherish thee, O precious pain?
Fain would my trembling hand
Fashion and forge of thee a deathless sword
To serve my stricken land!

And thou, sweet sorrow, terrible and dear,
Most bitter and divine?
O I will carve thee with deep agony
Into a deathless shrine!

# KALI THE MOTHER

*All Voices:*

    O TERRIBLE and tender and divine!
    O mystic mother of all sacrifice,
    We deck the sombre altars of thy shrine
    With sacred basil leaves and saffron rice;
    All gifts of life and death we bring to thee,
        *Uma Haimavati!*

*Maidens:*

    We bring thee buds and berries from the wed!

*Brides:*

    We bring the rapture of our bridal prayer!

*Mothers:*

    And we the sweet travail of motherhood!

*Widows:*

    And we the bitter vigils of despair!

*All Voices:*

    All gladness and all grief we bring to thee,
        *Ambika! Parvati!*

*Artisans:*

    We bring the lowly tribute of our toil!

*Peasants:*

> We bring our new-born goats and budded wheat!

*Victors:*

> And we the swords and symbols of our spoil!

*Vanquished:*

> And we the shame and sorrow of defeat!

*All Voices:*

> All triumph and all tears we bring to thee,
> *Girija! Shambhavi!*

*Scholars:*

> We bring the secrets of our ancient arts.

*Priests:*

> We bring the treasures of our ageless creeds.

*Poets:*

> And we the subtle music of our hearts.

*Patriots:*

> And we the sleepless worship of our deeds.

*All Voices:*

> All glory and all grace we bring to thee,
> *Kali! Maheshwari!* [4]

---

4    These are some of the many names of Kali the Eternal
Mother of Hindu worship.

# AWAKE!

_____

To Mohamed Ali Jinnah, Recited at the
*Indian National Congress,*
1915

WAKEN, O mother! thy children implore thee,
Who kneel in thy presence to serve and adore thee!
The night is aflush with a dream of the morrow,
Why still dost thou sleep in thy bondage of sorrow?
Awaken and sever the woes that enthrall us,
And hallow our hands for the triumphs that call us!

Are we not thine, O Belov'd, to inherit
The manifold pride and power of thy spirit?
Ne'er shall we fail thee, forsake thee or falter,
Whose hearts are thy home and thy shield and thine altar.
Lo! we would thrill the high stars with thy story,
And set thee again in the forefront of glory.

*Hindus:*

> Mother! the flowers of our worship
> have crowne thee!

*Parsees:*

> Mother! the flame of our hope shall surround thee

*Mussulmans:*

> Mother! the sword of our love shall defend thee

*Christians:*

Mother! the song of our faith shall attend thee!

*All Creeds:*

Shall not our dauntless devotion avail thee?
Hearken! O queen and O goddess, we hail thee

# THE
# FLOWERING YEAR

## THE CALL OF SPRING

---

### To Padmaja and Lilamani

CHILDREN, my children, the spring wakes anew,
And calls through the dawn and the daytime
For flower-like and fleet-footed maidens like you,
To share in the joy of its play-time.

O'er hill-side and valley, through garden and grove,
Such exquisite anthems are ringing
Where rapturous bulbul and maina and dove
Their carols of welcome are singing.

I know where the ivory lilies unfold
In brooklets half-hidden in sedges,
And the air is aglow with the blossoming gold
Of thickets and hollows and hedges.

I know where the dragon-flies glimmer and glide,
And the plumes of wild peacocks are gleaming,
Where the fox and the squirrel and timid fawn hide
And the hawk and the heron lie dreaming.

The earth is ashine like a humming-bird's wing,
And the sky like a kingfisher's feather,
O come, let us go and play with the spring
Like glad-hearted children together.

# THE
# COMING OF SPRING

O SPRING! I cannot run to greet
   Your coming as I did of old,
   Clad in a shining veil of gold,
With champa-buds and blowing wheat
And silver anklets on my feet.

Let others tread the flowering ways
   And pluck new leaves to bind their brows,
   And swing beneath the quickening boughs
A bloom with scented spikes and sprays
Of coral and of chrysoprase.

But if against this sheltering wall
   I lean to rest and lag behind,
   Think not my love untrue, unkind,
Or heedless of the luring call
To your enchanting festival.

O Sweet! I am not false to you—
   Only my weary heart of late
   Has fallen from its high estate
Of laughter and has lost the clue
To all the vernal joy it knew.

There was a song I used to sing—
  But now I seek in vain, in vain
  For the old lilting glad refrain—
I have forgotten everything—
Forgive me, O my comrade Spring!

*Vasant Panchami Day,* 1916

# THE
# MAGIC OF SPRING

---

I BURIED my heart so deep, so deep,
Under a secret hill of pain,
And said: "O broken pitiful thing
Even the magic spring
Shall ne'er wake thee to life again,
Tho' March woods glimmer with opal rain
And passionate koels sing."

The kimshuks burst into dazzling flower,
The seemuls burgeoned in crimson pride,
The palm-groves shone with the oriole's wing,
The koels began to sing,
The soft clouds broke in a twinkling tide . . .
My heart leapt up in its grave and cried.
*"Is it the spring, the spring?"*

175

# SUMMER WOODS

O I AM tired of painted roofs and soft and silken floors,
And long for wind-blown canopies of crimson *gulmohars!*

O I am tired of strife and song and festivals and fame,
And long to fly where cassia-woods are breaking into flame.

Love, come with me where koels all from flowering glade and glen,
Far from the toil and weariness, the praise and prayers of men.

O let us fling all care away, and lie alone and dream
'Neath tangled boughs of tamarind and molsari and neem!

And bind our brows with jasmine sprays and play on carven flutes,
To wake the slumbering serpent-kings among the banyan roots.

And roam at fall of eventide along the river's brink,
And bathe in water-lily pools where golden panthers drink!

You and I together, Love, in the deep blossoming woods
Engirt with love-voiced silences and gleaming solitudes.

Companions of the lustrous dawn, gay comrades of the night,
Like Krishna and like Radhika, encompassed with delight.

# JUNE SUNSET

HERE shall my heart find its haven of calm,
By rush-fringed rivers and rain-fed streams
That glimmer thro' meadows of lily and palm.
Here shall my soul find its true repose
Under a sunset sky of dreams
Diaphanous, amber and rose.
The air is aglow with the glint and whirl
Of swift wild wings in their homeward flight,
Sapphire, emerald, topaz, and pearl.
Afloat in the evening light.

A brown quail cries from the tamarisk bushes,
A bulbul calls from the cassia-plume,
And thro' the wet earth the gentian pushes
Her spikes of silvery bloom.

Where'er the foot of the bright shower passes
Fragrant and fresh delights unfold;
The wild fawns feed on the scented grasses,
Wild bees on the cactus-gold.

An ox-cart stumbles upon the rocks,
And a wistful music pursues the breeze
From a shepherd's pipe as he gathers his flocks
Under the pipal trees.
And a young Banjara driving her cattle
Lifts up her voice as she glitters by
In an ancient ballad of love and battle
Set to the beat of a mystic tune,
And the faint stars gleam in the eastern sky
To herald a rising moon.

# THE TIME OF ROSES

LOVE, it is the time of roses!
In bright fields and garden closes
How they burgeon and unfold!
How they sweep o'er tombs and towers
In voluptuous crimson showers
And untrammelled tides of gold!

How they lure wild bees to capture
All the rich mellifluous rapture
Of their magical perfume,
And to passing winds surrender
All their frail and dazzling splendour
Rivalling your turban-plume!

How they cleave the air adorning
The high rivers of the morning
In a blithe, bejewelled fleet!
How they deck the moonlit grasses
In thick rainbow-tinted masses
Like a fair queen's bridal sheet!

Hide me in a shrine of roses,
Drown me in a wine of roses
Drawn from every fragrant grove!
Bind me on a pyre of roses,
Burn me in a fire of roses,
Crown me with the rose of Love!

# THE
# PEACOCK-LUTE,
# SONGS FOR MUSIC

## SILVER TEARS

─────────────

MANY tributes Life hath brought me,
Delicate and touched with splendour . . .
Of all gracious gifts and tender
She hath given no gift diviner
Than your silver tears of sorrow
For my wild heart's suffering.

Many evils Time hath wrought me,
Happiness and health hath broken . . .
Of all joy or grief for token
He hath left no gift diviner
Than your silver tears of Sorrow
For my wild heart's suffering.

# CAPRICE

You held a wild flower in your fingertips,
Idly you pressed it to indifferent lips,
Idly you tore its crimson leaves apart . . .
Alas! it was my heart.

You held a wine-cup in your fingertips,
Lightly you raised it to indifferent lips,
Lightly you drank and flung away the bowl . . .
Alas! it was my soul.

# DESTINY

IT chanced on the noon of an April day
A dragon-fly passed in its sunward play
And furled his flight for a passing hour
To drain the life of a passion-flower . . .
Who cares if a ruined blossom die,
O bright blue wandering dragon-fly?

Love came, with his ivory flute,
His pleading eye, and his winged foot:
"I am weary," he murmured; "O let me rest
In the sheltering joy of your fragrant breast."
At dawn he fled and he left no token . . .
Who cares if a woman's heart be broken?

# ASHOKA BLOSSOM

---

IF a lovely maiden's foot
Treads on the Ashoka root,
Its glad branches sway and swell,
So our eastern legends tell,
Into gleaming flower,
Vivid clusters golden-red
To adorn her brow or bed
Or her marriage bower.

If your glowing foot be prest
O'er the secrets of my breast,
Love, my dreaming head would wake,
And its joyous fancies break
Into lyric bloom
To enchant the passing world
With melodious leaves unfurled
And their wild perfume.

# ATONEMENT

DEEP in a lonely garden on the hill,
　　Lulled by the low sea-tides,
A shadow set in shadows, soft and still,
　　A wandering spirit glides,
　Smiting its pallid palms and making moan
　*O let my Love atone!*

Deep in a lonely garden on the hill
　　Among the fallen leaves
A shadow lost in shadows, vague and chill,
　　A wandering spirit grieves,
　Beating its pallid breast and making moan
　*O let my Death atone!*

# LONGING

ROUND the sadness of my days
Breaks a melody of praise
Like a shining storm of petals,
Like a lustrous rain of pearls,
From the lutes of eager minstrels,
From the lips of glowing girls.

Round the sadness of my nights
Breaks a carnival of lights. . .
But amid the gleaming pageant
Of life's gay and dancing crowd
Glides my cold heart like a spectre
In a rose-encircled shroud.

Love, beyond these lonely years
Lies there still a shrine of tears,
A dim sanctuary of sorrow
Where my grieving heart may rest,
And on some deep tide of slumber
Reach the comfort of your breast?

# WELCOME

WELCOME, O fiery Pain!
My heart unseared, unstricken,
Drinks deep thy fervid rain,
My spirit-seeds to quicken,

Welcome, O tranquil Death!
Thou hast no ills to grieve me,
Who cam'st with Freedom's breath
From sorrow to retrieve me.

Open, O vast unknown,
Thy sealed mysterious portals!
I go to seek mine own,
Vision of Love immortal.

# THE FESTIVAL OF MEMORY

DOTH rapture hold a feast,
Doth sorrow keep a fast
For Love's dear memory
Whose sweetness shall outlast
The changing winds of Time,
Secret and unsurpassed?

Shall I array my heart
In Love's vermeil attire?
O shall I fling my life
Like incense in Love's fire?
Weep unto sorrow's lute?
Dance unto rapture's lyre?

What know the world's triune
Of gifts so strange as this
Twin-nurtured boon of Love,
Deep agony and bliss,
Fulfilment and farewell
Concentred in a kiss?

No worship dost thou need,
O miracle divine!
Silence and song and tears
Delight and dreams are thine,
Who mak'st my burning soul
Thy sacrament and shrine.

# THE TEMPLE,
# A PILGRAMAGE OF LOVE

## I. THE GATE OF DELIGHT

### 1.

---

### THE OFFERING

WERE beauty mine, beloved, I would bring it
Like a rare blossom to Love's glowing shrine;
Were dear youth mine, beloved, I would fling it
Like a rich pearl into Love's lustrous wine:

Were greatness mine, Beloved, I would offer
Such radiant gifts of glory and of fame,
Like camphor and like curds to pour and proffer
Before Love's bright and sacrificial flame.

But I have naught save my heart's deathless passion
That craves no recompense divinely sweet,
Content to wait in proud and lowly fashion,
And kiss the shadow of Love's passing feet.

## 2.

---

### THE FEAST

BRING no fragrant sandal-paste,
Let me gather, Love, instead
The entranced and flowering dust
You have honoured with your tread
For mine eyelids and mine head.

Bring no scented lotus-wreath
Moon-awakened, dew-caressed;
Love, thro' memory's age-long dream
Sweeter shall my wild heart rest
With your footprints on my breast.

Bring no pearls from ravished seas,
Gems from rifled hemispheres;
Grant me, Love, in priceless boon
All the sorrow of your years,
All the secret of your tears.

## 3.

---

### ECSTASY

LET spring illume the western hills with blossoming brands of fire,
And wake with rods of budded flame the valleys of the south —
But I have plucked you, O miraculous Flower of my desire,
And crushed between my lips the burning petals of your mouth!

Let spring unbind upon the breeze tresses of rich perfume
To lure the purple honey bees to their enchanted death —
But sweeter madness drives my soul to swift and sweeter doo
For I have drunk the deep, delicious nectar of your breath!

Let spring unlock the melodies of fountain and of flood,
And teach the winged word of man to mock the wild bird's
But wilder music thrilled me when the rivers of your blood
Swept o'er the floodgates of my life to drown my waiting heart!

# 4.

---

## THE LUTE-SONG

WHY need you a burnished mirror of gold,
O bright and imperious face?
Mine eyes be the shadowless wells of desire
For the sun of your glory and grace!

Why need you the praises of ivory lutes,
O proud and illustrious name?
My voice be the journeying lute of delight
For the song of your valour and fame!

Why need you pavilions and pillows of silk,
Soft foot-cloths of azure, O Sweet?
My heart be your tent and your pillow of rest,
And a place of repose for your feet!

Why need you sad penance or pardon or prayer
For life's passion and folly and fears?
My soul be your living atonement, O Love,
In the flame of immutable years!

## 5.

---

### IF YOU CALL ME

IF you call me I will come
   Swifter, O my Love,
Than a trembling forest deer
   Or a panting dove,
Swifter than a snake that flies
   To the charmer's thrall . . .
If you call me I will come
   Fearless what befall.

If you call me, I will come
   Swifter than desire,
Swifter than the lightning's feet
   Shod with plumes of fire.
Life's dark tides may roll between,
   Or Death's deep chasms divide —
If you call me I will come
   Fearless what betide.

# 6.

---

## THE SINS OF LOVE

FORGIVE me the sin of mine eyes,
O Love, if they dared for a space
Invade the dear shrine of your face
With eager, insistent delight,
Like wild birds intrepid of flight
That raid the high sanctuaried skies —
O pardon the sin of mine eyes!

Forgive me the sin of my hands
Perchance they were bold overmuch
In their tremulous longing to touch
Your beautiful flesh, to caress,
To clasp you, O Love, and to bless
With gifts as uncounted as sands —
O pardon the sin of my hands!

Forgive me the sin of my mouth,
O Love, if it wrought you a wrong,
With importunate silence or song
Assailed you, encircled, oppress'd,
And ravished your lips and your breast
To comfort its anguish of drouth —
O pardon the sin of my mouth!

Forgive me the sin of my heart,
If it trespassed against you and strove
To lure or to conquer your love
Its passionate love to appease,
To solace its hunger and ease
The wound of its sorrow or smart —
O pardon the sin of my heart!

# 7.

---

## THE DESIRE OF LOVE

O COULD I brew my soul like wine
   To make you strong,
O could I carve you Freedom's sword
   Out of my song!

Instil into your mortal flesh
   Immortal breath,
Triumphantly to conquer Life
   And trample Death.

What starry height of sacrifice
   Were left untrod,
So could my true love fashion you
   Into a God?

8.

---

## THE VISION OF LOVE

O Love! my foolish heart and eyes
Have lost all knowledge save of you,
And everywhere — in blowing skies
And flowering earth — I find anew
The changing glory of your face
The myriad symbols of your grace.

To my enraptured sight you are
Sovereign and sweet reality,
The splendour of the morning star,
The might and music of the sea,
The subtle fragrance of the spring,
Rich fruit of all Time's harvesting.

O Love! my foolish soul and sense
Have lost all vision save of you,
My sacred fount of sustenance
From which my spirit drinks anew
Sorrow and solace, hope and power
From life to life and hour to hour.

O poignant sword! O priceless crown,
O temple of my woe and bliss!
All pain is compassed by your frown.
All joy is centred in your kiss.
You are the substance of my breath
And you the mystic pang of Death.

# II. THE PATH OF TEARS

## 1.

_____

### THE SORROW OF LOVE

Why did you turn your face away?
　　Was it for grief or fear
Your strength would fail or your pride grow weak,
If you touched my hand, if you heard me speak,
　　After a life-long year?

Why did you turn your face away?
　　Was it for love or hate?
Or the spell of that wild miraculous hour
That hurled our souls with relentless power
　　In the eddying fires of fate?

Turn not your face from me, O Love!
　　Shall Sorrow or Death conspire
To set our suffering spirits free
From the passionate bondage of Memory
　　Or the thrall of the old desire?

## 2.

---

### THE SILENCE OF LOVE

SINCE thus I have endowed you with the whole
Joy of my flesh and treasure of my soul,
And your life debt to me looms so supreme,
Shall my love wax ungenerous as to seem
By sign or supplication to demand
An answering gift from your reluctant hand?

Give what you will . . . if aught be yours to give!
But tho' you are the breath by which I live
And all my days are a consuming pyre
Of unaccomplished longing and desire,
How shall my love beseech you or beset
Your heart with sad remembrance and regret?

Quenched are the fervent words I yearn to speak
And tho' I die, how shall I claim or seek
From your full rivers one reviving shower,
From your resplendent years one single hour?
Still for Love's sake I am foredoomed to bear
A load of passionate silence and despair.

# 3.

---

## THE MENACE OF LOVE

How long, O Love, shall ruthless pride avail you
Or wisdom shield you with her gracious wing,
When the sharp winds of memory shall assail you
In all the poignant malice of the spring?

All the sealed anguish of my blood shall taunt you
In the rich menace of red-flowering trees;
The yearning sorrow of my voice shall haunt you
In the low wailing of the midnight seas.

The tumult of your own wild heart shall smite you
With strong and sleepless pinions of desire,
The subtle hunger in your veins shall bite you
With swift and unrelenting fangs of fire.

When youth and spring and passion shall betray you
And mock your proud rebellion with defeat,
God knows, O Love, if I shall save or slay you
As you lie spent and broken at my feet!

## 4.

---

### LOVE'S GUERDON

FIERCE were the wounds you struck me, O My Love,
And bitter were the blows! . . .
Sweeter from your dear hands all suffering
Than rich love-tokens other comrades bring
Of crimson oleander and of rose.

Cold was your cruel laughter, O my Love,
And cruel were your words! . . .
Sweeter such harshness on your lips than all
Love-orisons from tender lips that fall,
And soft love-music of chakora -birds.

You plucked my heart and broke it, O my Love,
And bleeding, flung it down! . . .
Sweeter to die thus trodden of your feet,
Than reign apart upon an ivory seat
Crowned in a lonely rapture of renown.

## 5.

_____

### IF YOU WERE DEAD

IF you were dead I should not weep!
How sweetly would my sad heart rest
Close-gathered in a dreamless sleep
Among the garlands on your breast,
Happy at last and comforted
If you were dead!

For life is like a burning veil
That keeps our yearning souls apart,
Cold Fate a wall no hope may scale,
And pride a severing sword, Sweetheart!
And love a wide and troubled sea
'Twixt you and me.

If you were dead I should not weep —
How sweetly would our hearts unite
In a dim, undivided sleep,
Locked in Death's deep and narrow night,
All anger fled, all sorrow past,
O Love, at last!

# 6.

---

## SUPPLICATION

LOVE, it were not such deep unmeasured wrong
To wreck my life of youth and all delight,
Bereave my days of sweetness and to blight
My hidden wells of slumber and of song,
Had your atoning mercy let me keep
For sole and sad possession to assuage
The loss of my heart's radiant heritage,
Power of such blessed tears as mortals weep.

But I, O Love, am like a withered leaf
Burnt in devouring noontides of distress
And tossed upon dim pools of weariness,
Mute to the winds of gladness or of grief.
The changing glory of the earth and skies
Kindles no answering tribute in my breast,
My loving dead go streamwards to their rest
Unhonoured by the homage of mine eyes.

Restore me not the rapture that is gone,
The hope forbidden and the dream denied,
The ruined purpose and the broken pride,
Lost kinship with the starlight and the dawn.
But you whose proud, predestined hands control
My springs of sorrow, ecstasy and power,
Grant in the brief compassion of an hour
A gift of tears to save my stricken soul!

## 7.

---

## THE SLAYER

LOVE, if at dawn some passer-by should say,
" Lo! doth thy garment drip with morning dew?
Thy face perchance is drenched with cold sea-spray,
Thy hair with fallen rain? "
  Make answer: "*Nay* ,
*These be the death-drops from sad eyes I slew*
*With the quick torch of pain.*"

And if at dusk a reveller should cry,
" What rare vermilion vintage hast thou spilled,
Or is thy robe splashed with the glowing dye
Of some bruised crimson leaf? "
  O Love reply:
"*These be the life-drops of a heart I killed*
*With the swift spear of grief.*"

## 8.

---

## THE SECRET

THEY come, sweet maids and men with shining tribute,
Garlands and gifts, cymbals and songs of praise
How can they know I have been dead, Beloved,
These many mournful days?

Or that my delicate dreaming soul lies trampled
Like crushed ripe fruit, chance-trodden of your feet,
And how you flung the throbbing heart that loved you
To serve wild dogs for meat?

They bring me saffron veils and silver sandals
Rich crowns of honour to adorn my head —
For none save you may know the tragic secret,
O Love, that I am dead!

# III. THE SANCTUARY

## 1.

---

### THE FEAR OF LOVE

O COULD my love devise
A shield for you from envious lips and eyes
That desecrate the sweetness of your days
With tumults of their praise!

O could my love design
A secret, sealed, invulnerable shrine
To hide you, happy and inviolate,
From covetous Time and Fate.

Love, I am drenched with fear
Lest the uncounted avarice of the year
Add to the triumph of all garnered grace
The rapture of your face!

I tremble with despair
Lest the far-journeying winds and sunbeams bear
Bright rumours of your luring brows and breath
Unto the groves of Death.

What sanctuary can I pledge
Whose very love of you is sacrilege?
O I would save you from the ravening fire
Of my own heart's desire!

## 2.

———————————

## THE ILLUSION OF LOVE

BELOVED, you may be as all men say
    Only a transient spark
Of flickering flame set in a lamp of clay —
I care not . . . since you kindle all my dark
With the immortal lustres of the day.

And as all men deem, dearest, you may be
    Only a common shell
Chance-winnowed by the sea-winds from the sea —
I care not . . . since you make most audible
The subtle murmurs of eternity.

And tho' you are, like men of mortal race,
    Only a hapless thing
That Death may mar and destiny efface —
I care not . . . since unto my heart you bring
The very vision of God's dwelling-place.

## 3.

---

## THE WORSHIP OF LOVE

CRUSH me, O Love, betwixt thy radiant fingers
   Like a frail lemon leaf or basil bloom,
Till aught of me that lives for thee or lingers
   Be but the wraith of memory's perfume,
And every sunset wind that wandereth
Grow sweeter for my death!

Burn me, O Love, as in a glowing censer
   Dies the rich substance of a sandal grain,
Let my soul die till nought but an intenser
   Fragrance of my deep worship doth remain —
And every twilight star shall hold its breath
And praise thee for my death!

4.
_____

## LOVE TRIUMPHANT

IF your fair mind were quenched with dark distress,
Your dear hands stained with fierce blood-guiltiness,
Or your sweet flesh fell rotting from the bone,
Should not my deep unchanging love atone
And shield you from the sore decree of Fate
And the world's storm of horror and of hate?

What were to me your dire disease or crime,
The scorn of men, the cold revenge of Time?
Has life a suffering still I shall not dare,
Love, for your sake to conquer or to bear,
If I might yield you solace, succour, rest,
And hush your awful anguish on my breast?

## 5.

---

## LOVE OMNIPOTENT

O LOVE, is there aught I should fail to achieve for your sake?
Your need would invest my frail hands with invincible power
To tether the dawn and the darkness, to trample and break
The mountains like sea-shells, and crush the fair moon like a flower,
And drain the wide rivers as dew-drops and pluck from the skies
The sunbeams like arrows, the stars like proud impotent eyes.

O Love, is there aught I should fear to fulfil at your word?
Your will my weak hands with such dauntless delight would endow
To capture and tame the wild tempest to sing like a bird,
And bend the swift lightning to fashion a crown for your brow,
Unfurl the sealed triumph of Time like a foot-cloth outspread,
And rend the cold silence that conquers the lips of the dead.

## 6.

---

### LOVE TRANSCENDENT

WHEN Time shall cease and the world be ended
And Fate unravel the judgment scroll,
And God shall hear — by His hosts attended —
The secret legend of every soul,

And each shall pass to its place appointed,
And yours to His inmost paradise,
To sit encrowned " mid the peace-anointed,
O my saint with the sinless eyes!

My proud soul shall be unforgiven
For a passionate sin it will ne'er repent,
And I shall be doomed, O Love, and driven
And hurled from Heaven's high battlement,

Down the deep ages, alone, unfrightened,
Flung like a pebble thro' burning space;
But the speed of my fall shall be sweet and brightened
By the memoried joy of your radiant face!

Whirled like a leaf from aeon to aeon,
Tossed like a feather from flame to flame
Love, I shall chant a glorious paean,
And thrill the dead with your deathless name.

So you be safe in God's mystic garden,
Inclosed like a star in His ageless skies,
My outlawed spirit shall crave no pardon, —
O my saint with the sinless eyes!

## 7.

---

## INVOCATION

STOOP not from thy proud, lonely sphere,
  Star of my Trust!
But shine implacable and pure,
  Serene and just;
And bid my struggling spirit rise
  Clean from the dust!

Still let thy chastening wrath endure.
  O be thou still
A radiant and relentless flame,
  A crucible
To shatter and to shape anew
  My heart and will.

Still be thy scorn the burning height
  My feet must tread,
Still be thy grief the bitter crown
  That bows my head,
Thy stern, arraigning silences
  My daily bread!

So shall my yearning love at last
  Grow sanctified,
Thro' sorrow find deliverance
  From mortal pride,
So shall my soul, redeemed, re-born,
  Attain thy side.

## 8.

---

### DEVOTION

TAKE my flesh to feed your dogs if you choose,
Water your garden-trees with my blood if you will,
Turn my heart into ashes, my dreams into dust —
Am I not yours, O Love, to cherish or kill?

Strangle my soul and fling it into the fire!
Why should my true love falter or fear or rebel?
Love, I am yours to lie in your breast like a flower,
Or burn like a weed for your sake in the flame of hell.

CPSIA information can be obtained
at www.ICGtesting.com
Printed in the USA
FSHW011903030121
77366FS